David C. Cook
Lesson Commentary

BASED ON DAVID C. COOK ADULT CURRICULUM OUTLINES

Cook Communications Ministries Curriculum
Colorado Springs, Colorado / Paris, Ontario

Editor: *Bonnie Prestel*

Contributing Editor: *Dan Lioy*

Editorial Manager: *Doug Schmidt*

Cover Photography: © 1998 *by Dan Stultz*

Cover Designer: *Ty Pauls*

Contents

MARCH, APRIL, MAY 2005

Unit I: The Seeming Defeat

Unit II: The Captain Conquers

Unit III: The Team Cooperates

The Sheep and the Goats

Scripture

Background Scripture: *Matthew 25:31-46*

Scripture Lesson: *Matthew 25:31-45*

Key Verse: *"The King will reply, 'I tell you the truth, whatever you did for one of the least of these brothers of mine, you did for me.' " Matthew 25:40.*

Lesson Aim

To recognize the value of ministering to people in need and thereby glorify Christ.

Lesson Setting

Time: A.D. 30

Place: Mount of Olives outside Jerusalem

Lesson Outline

The Sheep and the Goats

  I. The Sheep and the Goats: Matthew 25:31-33
      A. *The Coming Judge: vs. 31*
      B. *The Determination: vss. 32-33*

 II. Those on Christ's Right: Matthew 25:34-40
      A. *The Promise of the Kingdom: vs. 34*
      B. *The Deeds of the Blessed: vss. 35-36*
      C. *The Questions Asked by the Blessed: vss. 37-39*
      D. *The Response Given by the Lord: vs. 40*

III. Those on Christ's Left: Matthew 25:41-45
      A. *The Pronouncement of Judgment: vs. 41*
      B. *The Failures of the Condemned: vss. 42-43*
      C. *The Questions Asked by the Condemned: vs. 44*
      D. *The Response Given by the Lord: vs. 45*

Introduction

Serving Christ by Serving Others

Several years ago when King Abdullah succeeded his father King Hussein on the throne of Jordan, he decided to discover the needs of his people. He assumed several roles in disguise, such as taxi driver, money changer, and so on. The people he worked with had no idea they were serving their king.

We recognize something similar taking place in Jesus' parable of the sheep and the goats. The sheep had no idea they helped Jesus, and the goats had no idea they refused to come to His aid. How many times do we make the same mistake? We simply do not recognize that by helping needy people, we are ministering to our Lord and King.

Lesson Commentary

I. The Sheep and the Goats: Matthew 25:31-33

A. The Coming Judge: vs. 31

"When the Son of Man comes in his glory, and all the angels with him, he will sit on his throne in heavenly glory."

Matthew 24:1—25:46 is the last of the five discourses in the first Synoptic Gospel. Because Jesus was sitting on the Mount of Olives when He taught this material to His disciples, it has been called the Olivet Discourse. It contains some of the most noteworthy prophetic passages in all of Scripture.

In 24:1-14, Jesus revealed the signs of His return. He then talked about perilous times (vss. 15-28) and the glory associated with His Second Coming (vss. 29-31). In the parable of the fig tree (vss. 32-35), Jesus said that as the buds of a fig tree tell that summer is near, so will signs tell that Christ's return is imminent. Then in verses 36-44, Jesus said that only the Father knew the time of His return. The coming of the Son of Man will be so sudden that the wicked and the righteous will be separated instantaneously.

Following the parable of the wise and wicked servants (vss. 45-

51), Jesus told three more parables related to His return: the parable of the 10 virgins (25:1-13), the parable of the talents (vss. 14-30), and the parable of the sheep and the goats (vss. 31-46). All of these stories have to do with being ready for Christ's return by being faithful to Him.

Each of these parables, however, has a slightly different slant. In the parable of the 10 virgins, Christ called His disciples to exercise foresight and wisdom as they prepared themselves for His return. In the parable of the talents, Jesus stressed that His followers were to be wise stewards of all He had entrusted to their care. And in the parable of the sheep and the goats, Jesus revealed that the righteous will be rewarded for their concern and hospitality, while the wicked will be punished for their indifference.

In the final parable that Jesus delivered on the Mount of Olives, He provided a few details about what His return will be like. First, Jesus will come in "glory" (vs. 31), or divine splendor, no longer simply appearing as an ordinary man. Second, He will bring with Him "all the angels," who will no doubt serve as His assistants. Third, Jesus will "sit on his throne in heavenly glory," meaning He will rule in splendor.

B. The Determination: vss. 32-33
"All the nations will be gathered before him, and he will separate the people one from another as a shepherd separates the sheep from the goats. He will put the sheep on his right and the goats on his left."

Once Jesus is seated on His throne, all the nations will be gathered in His presence. He will then separate them as a shepherd separates sheep from goats (Matt. 25:32). In other words, the purpose of the judgment will be to separate the righteous from the wicked. Only God can do that with perfect justice.

Shepherding was a prominent occupation in ancient Palestine. Shepherds had to make sure that their master's flock was provided for and protected. Shepherds would lead their animals to good pasturelands and ample supplies of water. They would find adequate shelter for their flocks and assist any crippled or exhausted animals. If necessary, shepherds would risk their own lives to ensure the safety of the flock.

Jesus compared the separation of humans to the way a shepherd would separate sheep from goats. In ancient Palestine sheep and

---

25:32 "Separate"

This word literally means "to mark off or set apart as if by a line or boundary." John the Baptist had proclaimed Jesus as the one who would separate the wheat from the chaff (3:12). The division of humanity that John prophesied is now depicted. The judgment of Jesus effects eternal destiny (v. 46).

goats often grazed together during the day. When night came, however, they were herded into separate folds. That was because the goats, unlike the sheep, could not easily endure the cooler night air and thus had to be grouped to keep warm.

The point of the comparison lies in the fact that sheep and goats were separated at the end of the day. As the shepherd of judgment, Jesus will put the "sheep" on His right and the "goats" on His left (vs. 33).

There are two primary ways of understanding Jesus' parable. Some say the "nations" (vs. 32) refer to all peoples, while others claim they refer to Gentiles only. One group thinks the judgment occurs at the conclusion of history; in contrast, the second group says it takes place when Jesus comes to set up a kingdom on earth. For those in the first group, the judgment determines who goes to heaven and who goes to hell. Oppositely, those in the second group say the judgment concerns who enters Jesus' earthly kingdom and who doesn't.

II. Those on Christ's Right: Matthew 25:34-40

A. The Promise of the Kingdom: vs. 34

"Then the King will say to those on his right, 'Come, you who are blessed by my Father; take your inheritance, the kingdom prepared for you since the creation of the world.' "

The remainder of Jesus' parable describes what He will do with the sheep (or the righteous) and the goats (or the wicked) once He has them separated. First He commented on the sheep (Matt. 25:34-40) and then the goats (vss. 41-45).

While seated on His throne, Jesus will reign as King and judge as King. He will address those on His right side as "blessed by my Father" (vs. 34). They will be favored by God in the blessing they will receive as an inheritance from Him, namely, the kingdom of heaven. Jesus described this Kingdom as having been "prepared for you since the creation of the world." All along it has been a part of God's plan to bless the righteous with His kingdom. Upon Christ's return, it will be time for the plan's fulfillment.

The kingdom of God embraces all who walk in fellowship with God and do His will. It is governed by God's laws, which are summed up in our duty to love God supremely and love others as ourselves. And this Kingdom, which was announced by the prophets and introduced by Jesus, will one day displace all the kingdoms of this world, following the return of Christ.

How can formerly sinful people share in the divine Kingdom? It's because they have trusted in God's Son, whom He sent to earth to die for humanity's transgressions (John 3:16). The believers' place in God's kingdom is assured because they are forgiven in Christ (Eph. 1:7). And their hope of salvation is sure because it rests on the work of Christ (1 Pet. 1:3-5).

B. The Deeds of the Blessed: vss. 35-36

"For I was hungry and you gave me something to eat, I was thirsty and you gave me something to drink, I was a stranger and you invited me in, I needed clothes and you clothed me, I was sick and you looked after me, I was in prison and you came to visit me.' "

Jesus said the righteous will inherit the Kingdom because of how they have treated Him. They will have met His needs for food, drink, shelter, clothing, nursing, and visitation (Matt. 25:35-36). These are things that anyone at any time in any society can understand, for they are the common concerns of life everywhere.

Thus, the test of faith that stands Christ's inspection will be how we performed deeds of mercy, love, and kindness. After all, this is what Jesus did for people while He was here on earth. And His righteous sheep follow His example. They show that their faith is practical and touches the lives of hurting people. Clearly, then, valid Christian faith is more than saying the right prayers or singing the right hymns. It includes standing alongside people in the harshest circumstances.

C. The Questions Asked by the Blessed: vss. 37-39

"Then the righteous will answer him, 'Lord, when did we see you hungry and feed you, or thirsty and give you something to drink? When did we see you a stranger and invite you in, or needing clothes and clothe you? When did we see you sick or in prison and go to visit you?' "

Jesus called His sheep "the righteous" (Matt. 25:37). They were upright because of their faith in Christ, and their lives were marked by righteous living because they cared for people in need.

The righteous ask a series of good questions in verses 37-39. In

5:37 "Righteous"

Righteousness was set forth as a distinguishing mark of disciples in the first sermon (e.g., 5:20; 6:1; 6:33). Those called "righteous" have followed this way of life. The focus of these verses, however, concerns simple acts of charity and hospitality given to those preaching the gospel (24:14) as representatives of Jesus (10:40-42). By their response to these messengers the righteous show their reception and acceptance of the gospel. By their indifference to them, the cursed show their rejection of this same message.

9

their spot, we too might wonder when we ever had an opportunity to do such things for Jesus. Here we see that Jesus wants us to show His love to others. Even the simplest act of kindness to the seemingly most insignificant person meets with God's approval and will be rewarded.

D. The Response Given by the Lord: vs. 40

"The King will reply, 'I tell you the truth, whatever you did for one of the least of these brothers of mine, you did for me.' "

Jesus said that the deeds the righteous had done "for one of the least of these brothers of mine" (Matt. 25:40) were done for Him. In other words, service done for Jesus' needy brothers and sisters is the same as service done for Him. This is an astounding truth, for it radically transforms our motivation for performing deeds of mercy.

There has been much discussion about the identity of the "brothers." Some have said they are the Jews; others say they are all Christians; still others say they are suffering people everywhere. Such a debate is much like the lawyer's earlier question to Jesus, "And who is my neighbor?" (Luke 10:29).

The point of Jesus' parable is not the who, but rather the what; in other words, the importance of serving where service is needed. The focus of this story about the sheep and the goats is that we should love every person and serve anyone we can. Such compassion and kindness glorifies God by reflecting our love for Him.

III. Those on Christ's Left: Matthew 25:41-45

A. The Pronouncement of Judgment: vs. 41

"Then he will say to those on his left, 'Depart from me, you who are cursed, into the eternal fire prepared for the devil and his angels.' "

Jesus next focused on the goats. Instead of being invited to come, like the ones on the right (the place of honor in ancient times), the ones on the left (the place of dishonor) will be told to depart. Instead of being blessed by the Father, these people will be cursed. Instead of inheriting the Kingdom prepared for the righteous, these people will be consigned to the eternal fire (hell) prepared for Satan and demons (Matt. 25:41).

25:40 "Least"

Although much debated (and often understood to be anyone in need), the clue to identifying these people seems to go back to the missionary discourse (10:5-42) especially 10:42. Related to that passage is the statement in this discourse (24:14) that the end will not come until the gospel is preached to "all nations." That the end has arrived (with Jesus' return and the judgment) means that the mission has been completed. What marks out the righteous (25:37) is their reception, care for, and identification with these missionary disciples regarded as "least" by the world but as the emissaries of Jesus by those who believe.

B. The Failures of the Condemned: vss. 42-43

" 'For I was hungry and you gave me nothing to eat, I was thirsty and you gave me nothing to drink, I was a stranger and you did not invite me in, I needed clothes and you did not clothe me, I was sick and in prison and you did not look after me.' "

Just as the righteous will inherit the Kingdom for meeting Jesus' needs, the wicked will be consigned to hell for not meeting His needs. They will have been presented with the same opportunities to give Him food and drink and the rest, but they will have chosen not to do so (Matt. 25:42-43).

For those who spurn Christ, all that remains is for the Lord to condemn them. It will be a terrifying scene as He issues a verdict of guilty against the unsaved.

C. The Questions Asked by the Condemned: vs. 44

"They also will answer, 'Lord, when did we see you hungry or thirsty or a stranger or needing clothes or sick or in prison, and did not help you?' "

The wicked will be just as mystified as the righteous about when they had the opportunities that Jesus mentioned. They will ask when they chose not to help the Lord (Matt. 25:44). They didn't realize that the basis for judgment will be whether they showed love to others, whom God has created in His image (1 John 3:14-18).

D. The Response Given by the Lord: vs. 45

"He will reply, 'I tell you the truth, whatever you did not do for one of the least of these, you did not do for me.' "

Christ's solemn reply will be that refusing to help others in need is the same as refusing to help Him (Matt. 24:45). Verse 46 concludes both the story of the sheep and the story of the goats. The wicked and righteous have radically different futures. The first group is eternally condemned, while the second group is eternally blessed. Jesus' judgments will be beyond appeal.

Discussion Questions

1. What will be the first thing Jesus does after sitting on His glorious throne?
2. What will be the destiny of those on Jesus' right?
3. What explanation did Jesus offer for this outcome?
4. What will be the destiny of those on Jesus' left? Why will this be so?
5. Which of our neighbors needs the touch of God's love through our hands?

Now Ask Yourself . . .

What side of Jesus will I be sitting on?
Am I prepared to stand at the Judgement seat of Christ?
How can I better serve my neighbors and friends in need?

Illustrations

As Jesus approached His crucifixion, He never wavered from judgment. He told His people to get ready, to keep watching, to keep working, and to take care of one another when they were hungry, sick, imprisoned, and so on. In fact, He pictured a grand finale of judgment when He will separate everyone, some to His kingdom and some to eternal fire.

We should not misinterpret the parable of the sheep and the goats to mean that one's eternal state is based upon good works. The New Testament is clear that faith in Christ (or its absence) determines our eternal destiny. Nevertheless, we can take away from this parable the ideas that Jesus rewards service done to Him, that real faith is expressed in works, and that He counts service done to His people as the same as service done to Him.

And what acts of service are they that receive the reward of the Kingdom? Included are simple things any of us can do— offering a meal to a hungry person and giving a cup of water to a thirsty person. Let's get busy! And let's get ready for Jesus to come!

There are 40 million children living on the streets of Latin America and over 1.5 million children on the streets of Manila in the Philippines. A lost generation to their countries. Lost to Christ.

Cross-cultural books that teach about God and his love for children are most effective and are used as a means of evangelizing and discipling children in the care of street children ministries. Cook Communications Ministries International has literature that can mean the difference between utter hopelessness or a life full of meaning.

To learn more about the global ministry projects of Cook Communications Ministries International, you can visit their web site at www.ccmi.org or call 1-800-323-7543.

Coming to Jerusalem

Scripture

Background Scripture: *Matthew 21:1-17*

Scripture Lesson: *Matthew 21:1-13*

Key Verse: *"Say to the Daughter of Zion, 'See, your king comes to you, gentle and riding on a donkey, on a colt, the foal of a donkey.' " Matthew 21:5*

Lesson Aim

To show more praise to Jesus and to acknowledge Him publicly as Lord and Savior.

Lesson Setting

Time: A.D. 30

Place: Jerusalem and nearby villages

Lesson Outline

Coming to Jerusalem

   I. Messiah's Triumphal Entry: Matthew 21:1-11

      A. *His Instructions: vss. 1-3*

      B. *His Humility: vss. 4-5*

      C. *The Crowd's Response: vss. 6-9*

      D. *The City's Response: vss. 10-11*

  II. Messiah's Cleansing of the Temple: Matthew 21:12-13

      A. *He Drove Out the Buyers and Sellers: vs. 12*

      B. *He Gave His Reasons: vs. 13*

Introduction

The Guidance of the Word

Pageantry excites people, whether it's a sports event, a political rally, an art or music fair, or even a religious event. In Christendom, Christmas, Easter, and Palm Sunday call for pageantry, including processions, music, and colorful banners. For many years, until politics intervened, the Palm Sunday procession leading from the Mount of Olives into Jerusalem was one of the most exciting religious processions anywhere.

Jesus did not avoid a wild public demonstration when the time was right according to his purposes. His triumphal entry, what we now call Palm Sunday, signified that He threw down the gauntlet to the nation of Israel. Would the people accept His coming as from heaven, from God above? Or would they see Him simply as another imposter, a false messiah?

This lesson forces us to examine our motives in coming to Jesus. If we join the crowd in hailing Jesus, we must accept all He has to offer and the changes He wants to make in our lives.

Lesson Commentary

I. Messiah's Triumphal Entry: Matthew 21:1-11

A. His Instructions: vss. 1-3

As they approached Jerusalem and came to Bethphage on the Mount of Olives, Jesus sent two disciples, saying to them, "Go to the village ahead of you, and at once you will find a donkey tied there, with her colt by her. Untie them and bring them to me. If anyone says anything to you, tell him that the Lord needs them, and he will send them right away."

According to Matthew's account of the life of Jesus, after His transfiguration He continued to teach His disciples as He moved toward Jerusalem. A number of explosive questions came up about such things as paying taxes, who would be greatest in the kingdom of heaven, what to do if you are sinned against, and divorce. Jesus also encountered a rich young man seeking eternal life and told him to sell all his possessions and follow Him. All the while he told the disciples what was coming: betrayal, condemnation, death, and resurrection.

In Matthew 21:1-5 we have one of the most specific fulfillments of Old Testament prophecy. Matthew's Jewish readers would undoubtedly be struck by the fact that Isaiah and Zechariah had given such a remarkable picture of this incident in the life of the Messiah. This would give the kind of confirmation they needed to show that Jesus of Nazareth really was the promised Messiah.

The triumphal entry began the last week of our Lord's life before His crucifixion. "As they approached Jerusalem" (vs. 1) includes the entire trip from Jericho to Bethany (John 12:1). They arrived Friday evening, had supper at the close of the Sabbath, and left Bethany on Sunday morning.

The immediate walk began from Bethany about two miles east of Jerusalem and led through Bethphage [BETH-fah-jee], a tiny village on the northern road over the Mount of Olives. This four-peaked hill stands 2,723 feet above sea level at its highest rising east of Jerusalem. It is separated from the city by the deep valley of the Kidron. It was named for olive orchards that formerly covered it.

The two disciples sent by Jesus are not identified by Matthew, so we guess they were Peter and John, who seem to have gone together on such errands. Their assignment was a strange one. Nothing like this had been requested before by Jesus.

The disciples could sense impending doom as they approached Jerusalem, based on what Jesus had told them, but we know from later events that they still were not prepared to accept His death. So they were probably trying to fit His request for the donkey and her colt into the melange of ideas accumulated over the past three years.

B. His Humility: vss. 4-5

This took place to fulfill what was spoken through the prophet: "Say to the Daughter of Zion, 'See, your king comes to you, gentle and riding on a donkey, on a colt, the foal of a donkey.' "

At this point Matthew explained that this event was the fulfillment of the prophecy of Zechariah 9:9. Israel's king would not come as a mounted warrior, but as a humble servant of the people. This was quite contrary to the popular expectations of the day. The people were looking for a military conqueror to overthrow their Roman overlords. They had failed to understand what their Scriptures taught about the Messiah.

Zion was the part of Jerusalem where David and the kings after him lived. "The Daughter of Zion" represented the people of the city. Jesus was indeed their king, and far more: He was the king of the universe.

Jesus taught and practiced humility. Gentleness was not the traditional quality of earthly rulers, who showed their power by ruthless vindictiveness. They often killed hundreds, even thousands, of innocent people to bring countries to fearful subjection. If they didn't kill them, they hauled them off into slavery.

Jesus was unmistakably different from human conquerors. His claim to sovereignty did not rest on political and military subjugation, but on strength of character and obedience to God's will. Nowhere did His distinctiveness become more apparent than when He rode into Jerusalem.

C. The Crowd's Response: vss. 6-9

The disciples went and did as Jesus had instructed them. They brought the donkey and the colt, placed their cloaks on them, and Jesus sat on them. A very large crowd spread their cloaks on the road, while others cut branches from the trees and spread them on the road. The crowds that went ahead of him and those that followed shouted, "Hosanna to the Son of David!" "Blessed is he who comes in the name of the Lord!" "Hosanna in the highest!"

The disciples did as Jesus had told them and found the donkey and the colt tied with her. No one had ever ridden the colt. The mare may have been brought along to keep her colt at ease.

Some of the disciples put their outer garments on the colt as a makeshift saddle. Jesus mounted the animal and started the steep ascent into the valley, a route that for years was jammed with thousands of pilgrims coming to Jerusalem for Passover. The climb from the valley into the city gate is more gradual.

His ride was a living parable, setting forth His claim to be King, God's Messiah. His kingdom was at hand, but what a different kingdom it was!—a kingdom of peace, love, humility, and gentleness. This king was gentle and peaceful, doing good to His enemies, bearing their persecutions with a gentle, forgiving spirit, even on the cross.

Somehow, a large crowd gathered at the Mount of Olives, sensing that something dramatic was about to happen. Of course, it included critics as well (Luke 19:39-40), but generally this was an emotionally charged multitude, full of high hopes as they came

---

21:9 "Hosanna"

This expression appears in the psalms of praise (Psalms 113-118) as an appeal to God for help or salvation. By this time, however, it seems to have become a word of praise or acclamation that was "familiar to everyone in Israel." Psalm 118 (v. 25 is cited) celebrates the faithfulness of God. Here the crowd acclaims Jesus as the Son of David voicing a truth few among them will firmly embrace.

from all over Israel and the world to celebrate the Passover. According to a census taken by the Roman emperor Nero, nearly three million Jews came to Jerusalem for the Passover.

A spontaneous outburst of adulation, welcome, and praise filled the air. People tore off their garments and threw them on the path. Others cut branches off the trees to cover the road. Spreading garments in front of an approaching king was a customary sign of tribute and allegiance. This was an ancient practice long before Sir Walter Raleigh took off his rich mantle and threw it into the mud for Queen Elizabeth to walk on.

Our practice of using palm branches on the anniversary of the triumphal entry comes from John's description of the event (John 12:13). Matthew, Mark, and Luke use different words: A young slip, a shoot, or twig (Matthew); a litter of branches and leaves (Mark); a mass of straw, rushes, or leaves beaten together or thrown loosely about, to form a bed or carpet (Luke).

The uproar soon focused on the shouts of "Hosanna!" This is a rendering into Greek letters of the Hebrew words, "Save us" (Ps. 118:25). This did not mean "Save us," but "God save the king." This cry reflected the deepest aspirations of the Jewish people, who, except for a brief interlude during the Maccabean rebellion, had been a subject people for 600 years. To have their own king and be set free was their centuries-old dream. Now it appeared that God had indeed heard their ancient cry.

"Hosanna in the highest!" means in the highest degree, in the highest strains, in the highest heavens. These were the manifold shouts of triumph, taken mostly from the 118th Psalm.

They saw the Son of David as the natural heir to the throne, the one who would inherit all of those glorious promises made to King David (2 Sam. 7:12-16; 1 Chron. 17:10-14). These people had a strong sense of history, which is still true in the Middle East today. They saw their King coming "in the name of the Lord," that is, sent by God and endorsed by Him as His representative.

D. The City's Response: vss. 10-11

When Jesus entered Jerusalem, the whole city was stirred and asked, "Who is this?" The crowds answered, "This is Jesus, the prophet from Nazareth in Galilee."

This stunning scene stirred up the whole city. This was a profound change for this city, used to pretenders, but not having a

17

clear picture about Jesus of Nazareth. Of course, some of them recalled His earlier visit, and many would have heard tales of His wonderful miracles in Galilee. But generally, in an age without media coverage, this event brought a huge uproar.

The word translated "stirred" means shaken as by an earthquake or a storm. It was used by Matthew to describe the effect of a violent storm on the waters of the Sea of Galilee (8:24).

The casual onlookers naturally wanted to know who was riding into the city with such a tremendous commotion. Most people did not recognize Jesus by sight, so the crowds had to identify Him. They called Him a prophet from Galilee.

For Jesus to enter Jerusalem like this required consummate courage. He was entering hostile territory as a rival King to the entrenched political and religious leaders. He was hated by the authorities, who, as we have seen, had long been plotting how to get rid of Him.

To make a dramatic appearance in such a way showed that Jesus was determined to make one last appeal against the indifference and incomprehension of the Jews. When His words and His miracles made little impact, He put His message and His Messianic claim into a dramatic public act.

Jesus did not sneak into Jerusalem under cover of darkness, but deliberately put Himself at center stage, forcing all eyes to be riveted on Him. He showed magnificent, sublime defiance to unbelief, unabashedly claiming to be the Lord's Messiah in the very minute details of the way He entered the city.

His courageous claim, however, was undergirded by love. His appeal was always to the heart. He blended perfectly boldness and gentleness as He provoked the city to answer the fundamental question, "Who is this?"

II. Messiah's Cleansing of the Temple: Matthew 21:12-13

A. He Drove Out Buyers and Sellers: vs. 12

Jesus entered the temple area and drove out all who were buying and selling there. He overturned the tables of the money changers and the benches of those selling doves.

The gentle prophet from Nazareth soon began acting quite differently. He made a dramatic appearance in the temple in

Jerusalem, obviously being followed by the tremendous crowds that had accompanied Him into the city.

They probably were expecting Him to assault the Roman authorities first, certainly not their own place of worship. This was a great time of preparation for the Passover, so the temple was filled not just with worshipers, but with those whose business it was to provide sacrifices—animals as well as doves—for them to offer. It was required that visitors to the feast purchase their sacrifices in Jerusalem.

Visitors came to Jerusalem with their own local money, so moneychangers had also become necessary. This was a profitable business, too, although apparently those working the temple precincts did not take exorbitant cuts.

In effect, Jesus claimed the temple as His own. He drove out those who had polluted it by commercializing it. No one stood in His way. This was the day of His triumph. This is how He showed what He had come to do, even in Jerusalem.

B. He Gave His Reasons: vs. 13

"It is written," he said to them, 'My house will be called a house of prayer,' but you are making it a 'den of robbers.' "

Jesus explained why He had taken such drastic action, by quoting Isaiah 56:7 and Jeremiah 7:11. Very simply, God's house of prayer had taken on the appearance of a den of robbers. Some of the business transactions were necessary for visiting worshipers, so what Jesus condemned was not the provision of sacrificial animals and local currency, but where all of this was taking place.

Apart from the temptations to exploit people economically, the whole character of the operation had radically changed what was supposed to be a spirit of penitence and prayer into something like a noisy flea market, where business rather than prayer prevailed.

21:13 "House of prayer"

Previously Jesus had warned his disciples about hypocrites who used prayer as a means to gain the praise of their fellow-men (6:5-6). Here he censures those who turn a place intended for prayer into a means of making a profit. Jesus had warned his disciples that they could not serve God and money (6:24). The temple leaders show their allegiance to money by permitting this disruption. The people had rightly hailed Jesus as a prophet (21:.11) and this cleansing is an act of prophetic censure.

Discussion Questions

1. What do you think the disciples thought about Jesus' plan to enter Jerusalem?
2. Why is it sometimes hard to understand and obey God's instructions?
3. What would you have done, had you been at the Mount of Olives that day? Why?
4. How can Christians show their exuberant, uninhibited praise of the Lord Jesus?
5. What impresses you most about Jesus on this occasion? Why?
6. When Christians are called upon to identify Jesus in a hostile environment, what should they say?

Now Ask Yourself . . .

Am I embarrassed to talk about Jesus in public?

How do my actions demonstrate the nature of Christ?

Does how I treat people make them want to praise Jesus?

Illustrations

Parades in honor of Jesus are out in most places today, but Christians still face the obligation to cry "Hosanna" whenever they can. Sometimes bringing praise to Jesus requires overt public action, even though it might be embarrassing. At such moments we have to recall the admirable courage Jesus exhibited.

On other occasions, however, our praise to Jesus might be inspired by our gentleness in the face of provocation. The church, rather than show its power and influence, might be more concerned about accepting the humility of Christ, even if it means being ridiculed.

The church has to reject political influence and the praise of the media, and follow the model of Jesus riding a donkey's colt. We also can bring praise to Jesus by the way we treat children and people with handicaps. He invited praise because of His outgoing love and care. He did not look down on the disabled, but healed them. He did not despise the cries of little children, but encouraged them. Perhaps if the church worked more at following Christ in these matters, He would receive more praise.

Death of Jesus

Scripture

Background Scripture: *Matthew 27:32-61*

Scripture Lesson: *Matthew 27:38-54*

Key Verse: *"Surely he was the Son of God!"*
Matthew 27:54b

Lesson Aim

To thank Jesus for dying for our sins.

Lesson Setting

Time: A.D. 30

Place: Jerusalem

Lesson Outline

Death of Jesus

   I. The Mocking of Jesus: Matthew 27:38-44
       A. *By the Crowd of Ordinary People: vss. 38-40*
       B. *By the Chief Priests, Teachers, and Elders:*
       vss. 41-43
       C. *By the Robbers: vs. 44*
  II. The Last Cry of Jesus: Matthew 27:45-50
       A. *"Why Have You Forsaken Me?": vss. 45-47*
       B. *He Gave Up His Spirit: vss. 48-50*
 III. Repercussions of His Death: Matthew 27:51-54
       A. *The Temple Curtain Was Torn and the Earth*
       Shook: vs. 51
       B. *The Dead Were Raised: vss. 52-53*
       C. *The Soldiers Confessed: vs. 54*

Introduction

Darkness before Dawn

The media are drawn to executions like bees to honey. The television cameras of today take the place of the hordes that used to jam the hill outside the Tower of London to watch criminals, political prisoners, and cast-off queens be hanged or beheaded.

Two thousand years ago, when Jesus was executed, the same public atmosphere prevailed. He was treated just like any other prisoner sentenced for His crimes. His executioners saw Him in the same light. No special treatment for God's Son.

At least Jesus was spared the ordeal of the ghoulish media flak. But He felt the pain, the shock, the humiliation that anyone else would. He also felt something no one else has ever felt: the crushing weight of taking the world's sin, guilt and judgment, thus being cut off from God, not for His own crimes, but for the crimes of others. Until people fully grasp why Jesus died for them, they will just be counted among the morbid curiosity seekers who flocked to Golgotha to watch Him die.

Lesson Commentary

I. The Mocking of Jesus: Matthew 27:38-44

A. By the Crowd of Ordinary People: vss. 38-40

Two robbers were crucified with him, one on his right and one on his left. Those who passed by hurled insults at him, shaking their heads and saying, "You who are going to destroy the temple and build it in three days, save yourself! Come down from the cross, if you are the Son of God!"

The last week of our Lord's life occupies about one-fourth of the record in the four Gospels, showing us how significant these events were regarded by the writers. At the same time, they did not dwell at length on Christ's physical sufferings unduly. They simply stated in brief, terse sentences what He endured. We must study and meditate on these facts, so we can better understand the meaning of Christ's death and grow in our own appreciation of His suffering on our behalf. Christians make much of the cross because it represents the outpouring of the Savior's love for them.

Jesus was arrested in Gethsemane and placed on trial before the Sanhedrin, the Jewish high court (26:47-68). After consulting among themselves, they delivered Him to Pilate, the Roman governor, and accused Him of many things. Jesus did not respond to their accusations (27:14)

Pilate bowed to the uproar of the crowd instigated by the chief priests and elders, freed Barabbas, and signed Jesus' death warrant (vss. 15-26). When Pilate saw that he could not prevail against the crowd, he tried to make public his own innocence of all that was to follow. In this strange, tragic scene, he washed his hands according to Jewish custom and placed responsibility for Christ's blood on the hands of others (vs. 24). It was a futile gesture. He could not escape his responsibility, even though the crowd willingly accepted the burden of Christ's blood.

Pilate then took the fateful step and turned over Jesus to be crucified. The preliminaries were every bit as dreadful as the act itself. The first step was scourging (vs. 26). The victim was stripped, tied to a post, and lashed with a long leather thong perhaps tipped with pieces of bone and lead pellets. Some victims died during this ordeal; most simply passed out.

Stripping Jesus of His own clothes, they put a scarlet robe on Him, probably belonging to one of the soldiers. They fashioned a crown to mock and punish Him. It was made of a common plant that had many small, sharp spines and soft, pliable branches. The leaves resembled a deep green ivy, an imitation of the victor's crown. For a scepter they handed Him a small piece of native papyrus bulrush that grew along the roadsides. Then they knelt before Him and shouted in false honor to the man they had heard identified as "King of the Jews." This means that they thought He was a self-deluded lunatic.

Our Lord's suffering at this point was both physical and emotional. It is hard to imagine the Lord of glory allowing Himself to be so humiliated, but this is exactly what happened. He took the form of a servant and "humbled himself and became obedient to death—even death on a cross!" (Phil. 2:8).

There was a triple execution on this day. The cross occupied by Jesus stood between crosses holding two robbers. This was the completion of our Lord's identification with sinners. Unknowingly, the pagan Roman officials were the means of fulfilling a Messianic prophecy given seven centuries earlier: the Messiah would be "numbered with the transgressors" (Isa. 53:12).

Throughout His ministry Jesus attracted throngs of people. His teachings and His miracles were not done in obscurity, but in full public view. Therefore, when His enemies succeeded in having Him killed, there were plenty of citizens ready to join the power-

---

27:38 "Robbers"

The picture of Jesus crucified with robbers on either side recalls his question to those who seized him in Gethsemane (26:55): have they come to arrest him like a robber? They had, and he here suffers the further indignity of being associated with criminals in his death. This picture also calls to mind the testimony of James and John that they would share the cup of God's wrath with him (20:22). Instead two robbers take their place. Rather than sharing his suffering, these two criminals amplify it with insults of their own.

ful, influential people.

The crowds followed the procession to Golgotha, and when they got there they hooted at Jesus. This was no time to take the stand in His defense. People were easily stampeded by blood lust. What better time to yell in derision than when the victim was helpless.

They hurled His own sayings back on Jesus, of course completely misunderstanding the words. The one about destroying and rebuilding the temple had been used against Him at His trial (26:61). The temple was the most sacred spot for the Jews and any thought of destroying it aroused their fury. But Jesus did not mean the temple building in Jerusalem. The saying was a prophecy of His own death and resurrection (see also John 2:19-22).

The people knew Jesus claimed to have come from God, so they challenged Him to prove it by coming down from the cross. Their demand only further revealed their unbelief. They had had ample chances to witness His divine power. Their taunt was one more strong temptation for Jesus to resist. He had faced this in Gethsemane, asking the Father for some way to avoid execution at Golgotha, but there was no way.

B. By the Chief Priests, Teachers, and Elders: vss. 41-43

In the same way the chief priests, the teachers of the law and the elders mocked him. "He saved others," they said, "but he can't save himself! He's the King of Israel! Let him come down now from the cross, and we will believe in him. He trusts in God. Let God rescue him now if he wants him, for he said, 'I am the Son of God.' "

The common people might have had some small excuse for being carried away at the execution of Jesus, but they deserved better from their spiritual leaders. The chief priests, teachers, and elders mocked Jesus because of the apparent inconsistency between His claim to be the Son of God and His helplessness on the cross. By their reasoning, if He were indeed the King of the Jews, the promised Messiah, He certainly would not be suffering humiliation and death. Therefore, they also challenged Him to save Himself and come down from the cross. They promised to believe in Him, if He would do that. No such miracle would happen, because they had already turned their backs on the light given to them by God. They had rejected God's Son at the very outset of His work, and they had been planning His demise all along.

Christ's obedience to His Father's will became the source of His torment. He obeyed without exception. At His trial no fault could be found against Him. Yet His critics sought to prove that God had deserted Him. By their logic, if Jesus were God's Son, the Father would rescue Him. God could not save Jesus from the cross that day and still be the holy, righteous, just God of the universe who forgives sinners. If Jesus had been rescued, sinners would have to die eternally as the just condemnation for their offense against God's righteousness and breaking His laws.

C.   By the Robbers: vs. 44
In the same way the robbers who were crucified with him also heaped insults on him.

They were bandits, possibly members of the gang of Barabbas. They were crucified with Jesus undoubtedly to add insult to His death and insult the Jews.

At first, both of the robbers joined in assailing Jesus. But as the day wore on, one of them—moved by the sublime attitude of Jesus and possibly by recalling His teachings and miracles—was actually converted (Luke 23:39-43). He rebuked the other robber for the abuse he was heaping on Jesus. Jesus assured the repentant robber that He would find forgiveness and a place with Him in Paradise.

II. The Last Cry of Jesus: Matthew 27:45-50

A.   "Why Have You Forsaken Me?": vss. 45-47
From the sixth hour until the ninth hour darkness came over all the land. About the ninth hour Jesus cried out in a loud voice, "Eloi, Eloi, lama sabachthani?"—which means, "My God, my God, why have you forsaken me?" When some of those standing there heard this, they said, "He's calling Elijah."

At noon, darkness enveloped Jerusalem for three hours. After six hours of excruciating pain, Jesus cried to God and asked why He had forsaken Him. Matthew recorded His words in Aramaic, the common language of the day.

Had God the Father really abandoned His Son in this hour of His darkest trial? Because of the unique relationship between the Father and the Son, we may never be able to grasp the depth of feeling behind Jesus' cry. However, we can be certain that His cry reflected the feeling that He was being forsaken on the cross. His cry also proves the terrible reality that at the moment—as Jesus

---

27:46 "Forsaken"

A quotation from Psalm 22 is the only record of Jesus' words from the cross in this gospel. These are the last words of his mortal life. In the words of the psalmist the reality of Jesus' death for the forgiveness of sins (26:28) is expressed. Bearing the sin of many, he is forsaken by God. The word means "to separate connection with someone". He drinks the cup of wrath that he prayed might be taken from him (26:39-44), the penalty for sin that ransoms many (20:28), and by so doing endures a separation from God. No other pain in his passion stands in comparison.

bore the sins of the world in His own body—God actually turned His back on His Son and abandoned Him.

It was necessary for Jesus to be abandoned by God on the cross. Since God by His nature cannot look upon sin (Hab. 1:13), He hid His face when our sins were placed on His sinless Son. Jesus was forsaken so that we might never be. "Never will I forsake you" (Heb. 13:5).

B. He Gave Up His Spirit: vss. 48-50

Immediately one of them ran and got a sponge. He filled it with wine vinegar, put it on a stick, and offered it to Jesus to drink. The rest said, "Now leave him alone. Let's see if Elijah comes to save him." And when Jesus had cried out again in a loud voice, he gave up his spirit.

Hearing His cry, some of the people thought Jesus was calling for Elijah (vs. 47). But one man ran, filled a sponge with wine vinegar, put it on a stick, and offered it to Jesus to drink. Then the people waited to see if Elijah would rescue Him.

It was commonly believed that Elijah would one day return to Israel. What better time for him to come than when the man who claimed to be God's Son was dying on the cross. "Let's see if Elijah comes to save him" was not a reflection of faith, but a callous call for another thrill. Because of the hardness of their hearts, they did not want any divine interference.

Jesus' cry—called the greatest single word ever spoken—is one word in Greek, but three in English: "It is finished" (John 19:30). To this Jesus added His prayer of dedication to His Father: "Into your hands I commit my spirit" (Luke 23:46). Jesus "gave up His spirit" before physical causes brought about His death. He did it at the moment of His own choosing. Most victims of crucifixion lingered for a day or more. That's what made the execution so horrible and why Pilate was surprised that Jesus died so soon.

III. Repercussions of His Death: Matthew 27:51-54

A. The Temple Curtain Was Torn and the Earth Shook: vs. 51

At that moment the curtain of the temple was torn in two from top to bottom. The earth shook and the rocks split.

God signified the meaning of Christ's death on the cross by tearing the temple curtain from top to bottom. After centuries of worship in the tabernacle and the temple, during which the Holy of Holies had been closed to everyone except the high priest on the Day of Atonement, now the way to God's presence was open to everybody.

The writer of Hebrews called this "a new and living way opened for us through the curtain" (10:20). It was opened by the blood of Jesus (10:19). The amazing application of this is that those who place their faith in Jesus can "draw near to God with a sincere heart in full assurance of faith" (10:22).

B. The Dead Were Raised: vss. 52-53

The tombs broke open and the bodies of many holy people who had died were raised to life. They came out of the tombs, and after Jesus' resurrection they went into the holy city and appeared to many people.

Because of a powerful earthquake, graves split apart and some people in them were raised to life. They were called "holy people," that is, people of faith and obedience to God.

Matthew added the fascinating detail (vs. 53) that those who had been raised on Good Friday went into Jerusalem after Easter Sunday "and appeared to many people." Probably they prepared the way for many people to believe in Jesus, after they learned that He, too, had been raised from the dead. It's also conceivable that those who came to believe formed the heart of the first church in Jerusalem.

C. The Soldiers Confessed: vs. 54

When the centurion and those with him who were guarding Jesus saw the earthquake and all that had happened, they were terrified, and exclaimed, "Surely he was the Son of God!"

Not all of the people mocked and derided Jesus. The Roman centurion, other guards, and some faithful, courageous women (vss. 55-56) stood apart from the mockery. The soldiers, who had seen everything, were significantly impressed by how Jesus had faced torture and death. The outcome was a strange confession for a Roman officer (Mark 15:39). He recognized that God was present in Jesus Christ. He did not possess full-blown theological understanding of Christ's relation to God, but he saw God's hand at work in the way Jesus died. Here was an unsolicited testimony to God's Son.

27:51 "Torn"

The death of Christ has several immediate consequences. Matthew records first the tearing of the curtain in the temple. Although this could be a reference to the curtain before the Holy of Holies (2 Chron. 3:14), it more likely refers to the great curtain that separated the sanctuary from the Court of Israel. Josephus describes this curtain which would have been visible to those bringing sacrifices to the great altar in the forecourt. Jesus has been accused (26:61) and mocked v. 40) for his prediction of the temple's destruction (24:2). This sign portends its eventual demise and serves as his preliminary vindication.

27

Discussion Questions

1. What emotions do you feel at the thought of the rejected King and Savior being tortured?
2. How does the cross of Christ become central in your worship, meditation, and daily conduct in the world?
3. How do you explain the intense hatred against Jesus, in view of all the words of love and deeds of mercy He had done for the people?
4. How do you account for the centurion's confession?
5. How do unbelievers mock Jesus? Why?
6. How should Christians react when they are ridiculed for their faith?

Now Ask Yourself . . .

Am I willing to suffer for my faith in Jesus?

When I am going through a painful trial in my life, do I blame God, or do I rejoice in my suffering?

Illustrations

We don't sing "The Old Rugged Cross" much any more, perhaps because it is an "emblem of suffering and shame." We've become so enamored with ideas of self-fulfillment and pleasure that we instinctively resist connecting suffering and shame with successful Christian living.

How unlike the Savior whom we profess to love and obey. Jesus willingly accepted the worst that sinful humanity could hurl at Him, even though He had legions of angels at His disposal to wipe them out. Today's popular psychology suggests that you are a fool if you do not use power to get ahead and to stick it to your foes.

Christians easily fall before the temptation to use power, to resist being tramped on or taken advantage of. Stick up for your rights and don't be a doormat, we are told. If the suffering of Jesus Christ before and during His crucifixion means anything, it is that we cannot, as Christians, follow the world's way of doing things. The church needs to recapture the spirit of "The Old Rugged Cross," not just the music but the words.

Jesus Crucified and Resurrected

Scripture

Background Scripture: *John 20:1-18*

Scripture Lesson: *John 20:1-18*

Key Verse: *"Don't be alarmed," he said. "You are looking for Jesus the Nazarene, who was crucified. He has risen! He is not here. See the place where they laid him."* Mark 16:6.

Lesson Aim

To thank Jesus for dying for our sins, and to tell the good news of His resurrection.

Lesson Setting

Time: A.D. 30

Place: Jerusalem

Lesson Outline

Jesus Crucified and Resurrected

I. The Empty Tomb: John 20:1-10
    A. *Mary went to the Tomb: vss. 1-2*
    B. *John and Peter Visit the Tomb: vss. 3-4*
    C. *What did they See?: vss. 5-7*
    D. *They Saw and Believed: vss. 8-10*

II. The Appearance of Jesus to Mary Magdalene: John 20:11-18
    A. *She Saw the Angels: vss. 11-13*
    B. *She Saw Jesus: vss. 14-16*
    C. *She Reported the Good News: vss. 17-18*

Introduction

From Death to Life

It was necessary for Jesus to die, so that He might bring us to glory, and so that He Himself might be crowned with glory and honor (Heb. 2:9-10). The necessity of His suffering eludes our rational thinking, just as the necessity of our suffering does. We would prefer a world free of pain and suffering.

The story of Christ's death proves that suffering precedes glory. His path is our destiny as well. The story of Christ's resurrection proves that glory follows suffering. Therefore, we live in the hope of our resurrection because Jesus lives.

The glorious news of Good Friday and Easter is that the penalty for our sins and our sinfulness has been fully paid, and that we may live forever with the Lord. This good news nourishes our souls, makes us better people, and prepares us for our eternal glory with Christ.

Lesson Commentary

I. The Empty Tomb: John 20:1-10

A. Mary went to the Tomb: vss. 1-2

Early on the first day of the week, while it was still dark, Mary Magdalene went to the tomb and saw that the stone had been removed from the entrance. So she came running to Simon Peter and the other disciple, the one Jesus loved, and said, "They have taken the Lord out of the tomb, and we don't know where they have put him!"

Good Friday gave way to Easter morning. That is the glorious news of the Gospel. Each Gospel account of the resurrection of Jesus gives a slightly different version of what happened, because each writer chose a different emphasis according to his purposes.

This chapter records three post-resurrection appearances of Christ. Each appearance brought about a different result in the lives of those involved.

John wanted to illustrate some of the spiritual lessons, so he includes the empty tomb, Christ's revelation to Mary, and her revelation to His disciples. Mary Magdalene's name probably derives from the town of Magdala in Galilee. he and a group of other women accompanied Jesus and His disciples. Because of her devotion to Christ, she witnessed His crucifixion and was concerned about anointing His body for burial.

It was still dark on the first day of the week when Mary went to the tomb and found that the stone had been rolled away. In her confusion and disappointment, Mary jumped to conclusions and assumed someone had stolen Christ's body. She ran to tell Peter and John ("the other disciple") who in turn visited the tomb.

B. John and Peter Visit the Tomb: vss. 3-4

So Peter and the other disciple started for the tomb. Both were running, but the other disciple outran Peter and reached the tomb first.

Why did John outrun Peter? (vs. 4) There may have been a physical reason: perhaps John was younger than Peter. But there is also a spiritual lesson here: Peter had not yet reaffirmed his devotion to Christ, and therefore his "spiritual energy" was low. Isaiah 40:31 says that those who hope in the Lord "will run and not grow weary," but Peter had rushed ahead of the Lord and disobeyed Him. Peter's sin affected his feet (John 20:4), his eyes (21:7), his lips (He denied the Lord), even his body temperature (18:18; and Luke 24:32).

C. What did they See?: vss. 5-7

He bent over and looked in at the strips of linens lying there but did not go in. Then Simon Peter, who was behind him, arrived and went into the tomb. He saw the strips of linen lying there, as well as the burial cloth that had been around Jesus' head. The cloth was folded up by itself, separate from the linen.

What did the men see in the tomb? They saw the burial wrappings lying in the shape of the body, but the body was gone! The graveclothes lay like an empty cocoon. The napkin (for the face) was carefully folded, lying by itself. It was not the scene of a grave robbery, for no robbers could have gotten the body out of the grave clothes without tearing the cloth and disarranging things. Jesus had returned to life in power and glory and had passed through the grave clothes and the tomb itself.

20:1 the "stone"

This would have been a disk-shaped "stone" that rolled in a groove. Some of these were large enough to require several men to roll them away from the entrance.

31

D. They Saw and Believed: vss. 8-10

Finally the other disciple, who had reached the tomb first, also went inside. He saw and believed. (They still did not understand from Scripture that Jesus had to rise from the dead.) Then the disciples went back to their homes, ...

Verse 8 tells us that the men believed in Jesus' resurrection because of the evidence that they saw. Later they met Christ personally and also came to believe on the testimony of Scripture.

There are, then, three types of proof that you can rest upon when it comes to spiritual matters: 1) the evidence God gives in His world, 2) the Word of God, and 3) personal experience. How can a man know that Christ is real? He can see the evidence in the lives of others; he can read the Word; and if he trusts Christ, he will experience it personally.

Note that in verse 10 they go back home without proclaiming the message of the risen Christ. Mere intellectual evidence alone will not change people. We must meet Christ personally.

That is what happened to Mary: she lingered and met Christ. How many times it pays to wait! (Prov. 8:17).

John said that he believed Jesus had been raised from the dead (20:8), but apparently the others did not.

Peter and John left Mary crying at the tomb. They returned to their secret hiding place in the city, but she stayed there, still thinking that Christ's body had been stolen. Then she decided to investigate the tomb herself, because to this point her conclusion was based only on the fact that the stone guarding the entrance had been removed.

20:12 Two "angels"

The "angels" themselves do not play a major role in John's account of Jesus' resurrection. They did not explain the significance of the empty tomb, but simply asked Mary the reason why she was weeping (v. 13).

II. The Appearance of Jesus to Mary Magdalene: John 20:11-18

A. She Saw the Angels: vss. 11-13

. . . but Mary stood outside the tomb crying. As she wept, she bent over to look into the tomb and saw two angels in white, seated where Jesus' body had been, one at the head and the other at the foot. They asked her, "Woman, why are you crying?" "They have taken my Lord away," she said, "and I don't know where they have put him."

Inside, Mary encountered two angels sitting on the slab where

Jesus had been laid to rest. Luke 24:4 calls them "Two men." The description of the angels in verse 12 reminds us of the mercy seat in the holy of holies (Exod. 25:17-19); the risen Christ is now our Mercy Seat in heaven.

Mary was overcome with grief, evidenced by tears. When the angels inquired about the reason for her tears, she simply blurted out her despair over the disposition of Jesus' body. "They have taken my Lord away" meant to Mary that His body had been taken to the Valley of Hinnom where the bodies of the crucified were thrown, eaten by vultures, and burned in the city's trash fires.

That's why she was crying. She could not comprehend how the one she was convinced was God's Messiah and her Lord could come to such an ignominious end. Mary then turned from the angels, for she was seeking Christ; she would have rather had the body of Christ than the sight of angels.

B. She Saw Jesus: vss. 14-16

At this, she turned around and saw Jesus standing there, but she did not realize that it was Jesus. "Woman," he said, "why are you crying? Who is it you are looking for?" Thinking he was the gardener, she said, "Sir, if you have carried him away, tell me where you have put him, and I will get him." Jesus said to her, "Mary." She turned toward him and cried out in Aramaic, "Rabboni!" (which means Teacher).

This is what Easter is all about. Through her tears Mary found the risen Christ. That is why Easter is such a poignant time for those who have lost Christian loved ones. They are reminded by Christ's resurrection that one day they will see their loved ones again, just as Mary saw Jesus again.

After answering the angels, Mary spoke to a man she thought was the gardener. He also noticed her tears and asked why she was weeping. Mary did not answer him, but bravely asked Him to tell her where He had taken her Lord's body. She was prepared to rescue His body and give it a proper burial.

The person she was speaking with was really Christ, but her eyes were clouded so that she could not recognize Him at first. Furthermore, she did not recognize Him because the idea that He was alive had never entered her head. Perhaps Jesus was not too different from the ordinary laborers of the day, despite how artists have depicted Him. At best, we can say she was psychologically blinded, and therefore found it impossible to recognize Him. The same thing happened to the two disciples who walked with the risen Christ on the way to Emmaus. Many Christians today are miserable because they assume something that is not at all true.

20:16 "Rabboni"

This is an Aramaic word (transliterated into Greek) meaning "my teacher" (an honorific title for a teacher of the Jewish Scriptures).

Finally, when Jesus spoke her name, Mary's eyes were opened and she recognized Him. Perhaps it was the more familiar tone of His voice that she recognized. He calls His own by name (John 10:3-4) and they know His voice (see Isaiah 43:1). She responded with the familiar endearing name she had called Him, "Rabboni."

Clouded by tears and despair, Mary's courageous faith brought her to this glorious recognition of the risen Christ. She loved Him so much that she was not afraid of guards, and was willing to carry His body by herself. Jesus responded to her faith, love, and courage by revealing Himself to her.

Jesus did not first go to Pilate and the Sanhedrin and say, "Aha, you thought you had me, but here I am!" He did not even go to Peter first.

Instead, he spoke to a woman who had come from a horrid background and honored her faith in a personal way. His resurrection is first personal, because He meets each one at our point of need. It was not ecclesiastical or political powers who needed to see Jesus first, but a humble woman of faith.

C. She Reported the Good News: vss. 17-18

Jesus said, "Do not hold on to me, for I have not yet returned to the Father. Go instead to my brothers and tell them, 'I am returning to my Father and your Father, to my God and your God.'" Mary Magdalene went to the disciples with the news: "I have seen the Lord!" And she told them that he had said these things to her.

Mary obviously worshiped Jesus and tried to grasp Him in an outpouring of Her affection. Jesus responded with two simple commands: "Do not hold me" and "Go to my brothers." Responsibility followed faith. She had to get back to the present world, so to speak. The glorious beauty of her encounter with Jesus in the garden did not last long.

Christ ascended to heaven to present His finished work to the Father. That secret ascension fulfilled the type of sacrifice discussed in Leviticus 23:1-14, the waving of the "firstfruits sheaf" the next day after the Sabbath (1 Cor. 15:23).

Mary had to know that He was now the risen Christ and that He would soon ascend to His Father. He was assuming a place of even greater glory and authority. Mary could not hold Him to this earth and reclaim their old relationship.

She was to tell His disciples about His destiny. He would regain the power and authority He had relinquished when He became the Son of God incarnate. Mary obeyed Jesus implicitly, first giving her simple testimony, "I have seen the Lord," and then reporting what He had told her. Mary's meeting with Christ made her a missionary!

Easter is the Church's declaration that Christ is alive, we have seen Him by faith. We believe that He holds full authority and power with His Father in heaven.

Discussion Questions

1. What impresses you most about Christ's suffering and death?
2. What should our first and continuing response be to the fact that Jesus died for us? Why?
3. Since the biblical writers give sparse details about Christ's suffering, what value is there in contemplating His physical sufferings?
4. Why were the disciples not prepared to accept Christ's resurrection?
5. What difference did Mary's courage and testimony make?
6. How can Christians today be more courageous in their witness to Christ?

Now Ask Yourself . . .

How can I be courageous in my faith?

Can I trust in things I cannot see with my physical eyes?

Will I trust Jesus with my life?

Illustrations

The Church must talk about life and death. Sadly, it seems, people talk more about death, mostly because the world at large tries to avoid it by any means possible.

The latest health care discovery earns a segment on television newscasts. We spend billions trying to stay well and to look good. But we cannot postpone the inevitable. Therefore, the Church must declare that there is something more important than avoiding death, and that is entering life that will never end.

God warns us that death comes to all. It even came to His Son on Good Friday.

Christians observe the day because it tells them the awful consequences of their sins. The Cross remains central to our thinking and our message.

But God also tells us about life. Death is not the end. Easter follows Good Friday. The world desperately needs the good news about life that can be eternal because Jesus rose from the dead. Every Christian must call to a dying world, "Receive life!"

Jesus Lives!

Scripture

Background Scripture: *Luke 24:13-32*
Scripture Lesson: *Luke 24:13-27, 30-32*
Key Verse: *"They asked each other, "Were not our hearts burning within us while he talked with us on the road and opened the Scriptures to us?" Luke 24:32.*

Lesson Aim

Understanding the Scriptures helps people come to know the living Savior.

Lesson Setting

Time: A.D. 30
Place: The road to Emmaus

Lesson Outline

Jesus Lives!

   I. Walking with the Savior: Luke 24:13-16
       A. *The Two Disciples Discuss Recent Events:*
          vss. 13-14
       B. *The Savior Appears: vss. 15-16*
  II. Talking with the Savior: Luke 24:17-27
       A. *The First Question and Response: vss. 17-18*
       B. *The Second Question and Response: vss. 19-24*
       C. *The Savior's Explanation: vss. 25-27*
 III. Sharing a Meal with the Savior: Luke 24:30-32

Introduction

He Has Risen

Because of its unique role in the Christian faith, Jesus' resurrection has become a special target of skeptics. They do not deny the historical fact that Jesus died, for they recognize that all people die. Instead, they reject the Christian teaching that Jesus was raised from the dead. The doctrine of the Resurrection is a problem for many of these critics because it stands in opposition to their belief in the finality of death and freedom from divine accountability.

The four Gospel writers perhaps sensed that critics, who depended on human reasoning, would leave no stone unturned as they mounted their attacks against the proclamation of Jesus' bodily resurrection. Thus in their own unique ways, Matthew, Mark, Luke, and John included accurate accounts of what took place at Calvary and thereafter. They have provided all the important facts about what happened to Jesus.

This week's lesson concerns the living Savior's encounter with the two disciples walking along the road to Emmaus. We will learn not only that Jesus died on the cross but also that He truly rose from the dead and lives today.

Lesson Commentary

I. Walking with the Savior: Luke 24:13-16

A. The Two Disciples Discuss Recent Events: vss. 13-14

Now that same day two of them were going to a village called Emmaus, about seven miles from Jerusalem. They were talking with each other about everything that had happened.

At dawn on the first day of the week, Jesus rose from the dead (Luke 24:1-12). Then later that same day two of Jesus' followers were walking to a village called Emmaus, which Luke said was about seven miles (possibly northwest) from Jerusalem (vs. 13). Although many towns have been suggested as the original site of Emmaus, the exact location remains unknown.

The pair was talking to each other about the things that had recently happened to their Lord. They were undoubtedly preoccupied with the execution of their Savior. They probably also discussed the report of the empty tomb and the news that He had risen from the dead. As they walked, they conversed about the recent events and discussed what they might mean. They did the best they could with the limited knowledge they had, but they lacked the key that would unlock the prophetic Scriptures: the Messiah must suffer and die before He could enter into His glory. It was this key that Jesus provided as He walked and talked with them on the road.

B. The Savior Appears: vss. 15-16

As they talked and discussed these things with each other, Jesus himself came up and walked along with them; but they were kept from recognizing him.

The words rendered "talked and discussed" (Luke 24:15) suggests the two disciples were having a heated discussion. Then, at some point Jesus personally drew near to them and began to walk with them (Luke 24:15). The pair, however, did not recognize Him.

It is not clear what kept the two from identifying the Messiah. Some suggest the pair did not get a good look at Jesus as they walked toward the west, perhaps into a sinking sun (see vs. 29). Others think the Lord supernaturally prevented them from knowing that it was Him. And there are those who speculate the disciples could not believe that Jesus was still alive.

These two men were "slow of heart to believe all that the prophets have spoken" (vs. 25). They believed the promises about Messiah's glory, but they could not accept the prophecies about His suffering (1 Peter 1:8-12).

II. Talking with the Savior: Luke 24:17-27

A. The First Question and Response: vss. 17-18

He asked them, "What are you discussing together as you walk along?" They stood still, their faces downcast. One of them, named Cleopas, asked him, "Are you only a visitor to Jerusalem and do not know the things that have happened there in these days?"

Jesus asked the two disciples what they were discussing so intently between themselves (Luke 24:17). The Savior's question prompted them to stop walking. At that moment, sadness clouded their faces. Undoubtedly, the recent demise of their Lord had been the focus of their conversation.

24:16 "From recognizing"

Luke does not explain how they could not recognize Jesus. It is clear that though Jesus is raised bodily, that body has a different quality than normal flesh. These two will not figure out who Jesus is until much later (24:31). The timing is partly seen as a divine work, as their eyes were kept from recognizing him now, but will be opened when they recognize him later.

Verse 18 identifies one of the disciples as Cleopas. All attempts to identify him further have been unsuccessful. He apparently was a faithful follower of Jesus, for he was present with the disciples in the upper room when the women reported on their trip to the empty tomb (vs. 23). We have no information at all on the other disciple. Possibly this person was the wife of Cleopas, since it appears they lived at the same place (vss. 28-29). But it is also possible that the traveling companion of Cleopas was his son, his brother, or his friend.

Some have suggested the two disciples may have been with other followers of Jesus who went to Jerusalem during the time of the Passover. If so, the pair would have been with the crowds as they extolled the Savior on His triumphal entry into the holy city (19:39). Now the two were returning to their home in Emmaus.

According to 24:18, Cleopas assumed that the person who had just joined the pair was ignorant of what had happened in Jerusalem over the past few days. With open-mouthed wonder Cleopas asked whether He was a visitor who did not know what had recently occurred. The disciple was suggesting that only a person who had lived elsewhere could be ignorant of the fact that the Jewish and Roman authorities had crucified Jesus of Nazareth.

B. The Second Question and Response: vss. 19-24

"What things?" he asked. "About Jesus of Nazareth," they replied. "He was a prophet, powerful in word and deed before God and all the people. The chief priests and our rulers handed him over to be sentenced to death, and they crucified him; but we had hoped that he was the one who was going to redeem Israel. And what is more, it is the third day since all this took place. In addition, some of our women amazed us. They went to the tomb early this morning but didn't find his body. They came and told us that they had seen a vision of angels, who said he was alive. Then some of our companions went to the tomb and found it just as the women had said, but him they did not see."

By asking the two disciples "What things?" (Luke 24:19), Jesus invited them to share all they knew about the Savior. As they talked, they revealed the extent of their ignorance and their need to learn more about Him from the Scripture.

The pair reviewed the main points of their conversation, which had been about the significant events that had taken place in the life of Jesus of Nazareth. During the time of Christ, Nazareth was a small town in southern Galilee. It was located in a mountain range overlooking the Plain of Esdraelon, which lay about 1,000 feet below. The Sea of Galilee, 15 miles to the east, the Mediterranean Sea, 20 miles due west, and Mount Hermon, 60 miles northeast, were all visible from the hill behind Nazareth.

The disciples referred to Jesus as a prophet—that is, someone, who officially spoke for and represented God. They also explained that Jesus was no ordinary prophet, for He had been uniquely blessed by God and had attracted the affection of many Jewish people. Perhaps there was sadness in their voices as the pair shared how the nation's religious and political leaders had plotted Jesus' death and had handed Him over to the Romans to be crucified (vs. 20).

Like many followers of Christ, these two evidently had hoped the Savior would liberate Israel and free their nation from the political and military control of Rome (vs. 21). All such thinking, however, was misguided and revealed just how ignorant they were of what Jesus had come to do. The pair noted that it was now the third day since Jesus had been executed. The doubts of the two disciples are made clear by the astonishment they felt when they had heard the report of the women (vs. 22).

Earlier that Sunday morning the women had been at the tomb and had seen that Jesus' body was not there. God had sent angels to tell these women that Christ was alive. After this, Peter and John had gone to the tomb to investigate what the women had said about the Messiah. They discovered that the testimony of the women was true (vss. 23-24).

24:25 "Slow"

Their hesitation to believe earns the two disciples a rebuke from Jesus. He calls them "slow of heart" (or dull of heart) to believe all the prophets have spoken.

What has taken place is a realization of things predicted in the Scriptures.

C. The Savior's Explanation: vss. 25-27

He said to them, "How foolish you are, and how slow of heart to believe all that the prophets have spoken! Did not the Christ have to suffer these things and then enter his glory?" And beginning with Moses and all the Prophets, he explained to them what was said in all the Scriptures concerning himself.

In calling the two disciples "foolish" (Luke 24:25), Jesus was underscoring their lack of spiritual insight regarding Himself and the true nature of His redemptive mission on earth. They had not understood the truths that the Old Testament prophets had declared about the Messiah. Since the pair had tunnel vision, it impaired their ability to grasp the necessity of Jesus' death. Consequently, He emphasized to them that it was God's will for the Redeemer to suffer before His resurrection from the dead and entrance into His glory (vs. 26).

Now that the Savior was again alive, it was imperative for His followers to fully grasp what had taken place, what He had taught, and what the prophets had foretold about Him. Jesus thus took the time to explain to the two disciples the meaning of key passages from the Hebrew Scriptures (vs. 27). The phrase "beginning with Moses and all the Prophets" was Luke's way of referring to pertinent passages throughout the Old Testament. By methodically reviewing the major Bible verses pertaining to His work on the cross, Jesus helped the pair understand who He truly was.

III. Sharing a Meal with the Savior: Luke 24:30-32

When he was at the table with them, he took bread, gave thanks, broke it and began to give it to them. Then their eyes were opened and they recognized him, and he disappeared from their sight. They asked each other, "Were not our hearts burning within us while he talked with us on the road and opened the Scriptures to us?"

It was now late in the afternoon as the three travelers reached the outskirts of Emmaus, and Jesus acted as though He would continue on His way. But in keeping with ancient practices of hospitality, the pair urged Him to spend the night with them. Thus Jesus accepted their invitation (vs. 28-29).

When the three sat together to eat the evening meal, Jesus took a small loaf of bread, asked God's blessing on it, broke it, and began to give it to the two disciples (vs. 30). In that moment they realized the Savior's identity. We can only guess what triggered their recognition. Was it the way Jesus prayed for the meal? Did the two suddenly recall how He had broken bread for the five thousand? Did they see the nail scars in His hands?

Jesus opened their eyes and hearts to understand all the Scriptures, and this brought a warmth to their hearts (v. 32). They saw Messiah in the Word, but they did not realize He was walking with them! It was not until He blessed their simple meal that Jesus revealed Himself to them personally. What a revelation! It transformed them from discouraged pilgrims into enthusiastic witnesses!

As soon as the pair knew Jesus was with them, He vanished from their sight (vs. 31). Then they began to understand, and hope sparked within them. They felt as though their hearts were on fire with new life (vs. 32). Because they had opened their hearts to the Lord, He opened their understanding. And though it was late, the two couldn't wait to tell the other disciples back in Jerusalem what had happened. Thus, they hurried out into the night, prepared to hike seven miles through darkness, to herald the good news of the living Savior (vs. 33).

24:32 "Burn"

This term normally refers to lighting a lamp, which gives off a burning light. This is the only use of this term with a figurative meaning in the New Testament. To speak of hearts burning is to speak of being moved by something.

Discussion Questions

1. Why do you think the disciples did not initially recognize Jesus?
2. What does the sadness of the disciples indicate about their faith in Christ?
3. Why did Jesus call the two disciples foolish?
4. What role did the Scriptures play in helping the two disciples learn more about the Savior?
5. If you had been one of the two disciples on the road to Emmaus, what things about Jesus do you think you would have been talking about?

Now Ask Yourself . . .

What was the best news I ever heard? How long did it take me to believe it?

What can I do to set aside preconceived notions about Jesus before I read God's Word?

In times of discouragement, how can knowing the Savior better through His Word help me to become more hopeful?

Illustrations

Books! Books! Books! Hardcovers and paperbacks; reference works and joke books; romantic novels and mysteries; self-help books and religious publications. They just keep appearing, and we keep buying them. There is one book, however, that surpasses all the others that have been or will be written—the Bible. In it we learn about the Savior's birth, death, and resurrection. From Scripture we also discover that the Messiah lives in all believers and promises them an eternal home in heaven.

As Jesus shared various passages of Scripture with the two disciples, He helped them gain a better understanding of why He had to die on the cross. We also can learn more about the Savior as we spend time studying the Bible. When questions concerning Jesus puzzle us, we can draw upon God's Word for clarification. Our faith in Him will be enhanced and our understanding of what He did for us on the cross will be improved. As we delve into Scripture, we will be better prepared to answer questions we might have about the Messiah and that others might ask about Him.

The knowledge of Christ that we have obtained from studying the Bible can serve as a spiritual anchor when our lives are filled with turmoil and doubt. Similarly, our understanding of what the Bible teaches about the Savior can be used to encourage other Christians who are discouraged or distressed. We can draw on our knowledge of Christ when we are combating false teaching about Him or alerting our fellow believers of erroneous ideas others are spreading. Finally, we can help new converts learn more about the Savior by teaching them the rich truths we have learned from Scripture.

Jesus Appeared to His Disciples

Scripture

Background Scripture: *John 20:19-29*

Scripture Lesson: *John 20:19-29*

Key Verse: *Then Jesus told him, "Because you have seen me, you have believed; blessed are those who have not seen and yet have believed" John 20:29*

Lesson Aim

To meet Jesus personally, confess Him as God and my Lord, and engage in His world mission.

Lesson Setting

Time: A.D. 30

Place: Jerusalem

Lesson Outline

Jesus Appeared to His Disciples

   I.   The Disciples Saw Him: John 20:19-20
    A. *They Were Fearful: vs. 19a*
    B. *Jesus Spoke Peace: vs. 19b*
    C. *They Were Glad: vs. 20*
  II.   The Disciples Were Commissioned: John 20:21-23
    A. *Jesus Sent Them: vs. 21*
    B. *Jesus Promised the Holy Spirit: vs. 22*
    C. *Jesus Gave Authority: vs. 23*
 III.   The Case of Thomas: John 20:24-29
    A. *He Did Not Believe: vss. 24-25*
    B. *Jesus Appeared Again: vs. 26*
    C. *Jesus Invited Thomas: vs. 27*
    D. *Thomas Confessed: vs. 28*
    E. *Jesus Encouraged Faith: vs. 29*

Introduction

Believing without Seeing

No resurrection, no mission. The church's world mission explodes from the dramatic news that Jesus lives. The church advances on His resurrection power. The apostle Paul began the church's great missionary movement convinced that the risen Christ lived in him and energized him.

That's why it is so important to settle the issue of who Jesus is the way Thomas settled it. Unless a person is really convinced that Jesus is God, no church can inspire obedience to Christ's Great Commission.

Every Christian, having met Christ, must ask the next question: "What do You want me to do, Lord?" This is the product of genuine conversion. This lesson shows that ultimately we offer Jesus all we have and are, or we give Him nothing.

Lesson Commentary

I. The Disciples Saw Him: John 20:19-20

A. They Were Fearful: vs. 19a

On the evening of that first day of the week, when the disciples were together, with the doors locked for fear of the Jews, . . .

Our story of Christ's resurrection picks up after the discovery of the empty tomb and the recovery of the grave clothes (John 20:1-7). Meanwhile, the disciples went home and Jesus appeared to Mary Magdalene (last week's study). She then told the disciples that she had seen Jesus (20:18).

John highlighted their prevailing fear. They were hiding behind locked doors in some secret hiding place, perhaps the upper room where they had met with Jesus previously. Most of them had fled when Jesus was crucified. Of course, their fears were well taken, because the Sanhedrin could easily have had them rounded up and executed as traitors to Rome.

In addition to fear, they suffered horrendous grief, so they were still in the shock of mourning. The Feast of Unleavened Bread was still going on, so they would not have left Jerusalem for Galilee anyway. The time of the Resurrection was the "first day of the week." That's why the early Christians changed their day of worship from the Sabbath (the seventh day) to Sunday.

Although the disciples' fear was warranted by the hostility surrounding them, we also have to note that Jesus had prepared them for this. When He described His death to them, He explained that

He would be raised from the dead (Matt. 16:21, for example). But just as they had resisted the idea of His death, so they could not comprehend His resurrection. So even though Mary had told them Jesus was alive, they were still overcome by their fears.

B. Jesus Spoke Peace: vs. 19b

. . . Jesus came and stood among them and said, "Peace be with you!"

Prior to entering the room, Jesus had appeared to the women returning from the tomb (Matt. 28:8-10), to Peter (Luke 24:34), and to the Emmaus disciples (Luke 24:13-33). Of course, the locked door did not stop Jesus from coming in. In His resurrection body, Jesus appeared wherever He wanted to—without physical limitations.

Of course, suddenly seeing someone in the room who had walked in through the locked door was a further shock. This had to be a spirit of some kind. Therefore, knowing their terror, Jesus first spoke peace to His friends. This was a standard Jewish blessing, something like "God bless you." But this was not a meaningless formal greeting. Jesus really wanted to give them peace. He had promised them peace (John 14:27) and now He gave them peace—that is, calmness, self-composure, freedom from terror.

C. They Were Glad: vs. 20

After he said this, he showed them his hands and side. The disciples were overjoyed when they saw the Lord.

However, His appearance and His words were not enough to settle them. So Jesus gave them the clear-cut evidence of His wounds—His nail-pierced hands and His spear-pierced side. That was what they needed. Their fears subsided and turned to joy.

Perhaps they should have believed the reports, but because of the depth of their despair and sorrow, they needed to see actual evidence of Christ's resurrection for themselves. Their shock was so great that they needed strong assurance. They could not deny Christ's scars when they saw them.

They also needed reassurance that they were not seeing a ghost or disembodied spirit. Christ's resurrection body was a real body, demonstrated by His eating food (Luke 24:42-43; John 21:11-15).

John's concern was with the spiritual shape of the disciples. They were glad when they recognized Jesus. He was the answer to their depleted faith. Their faith and understanding were growing, and they expressed their joy at the wonderful realization of Christ's resurrection.

II. The Disciples Were Commissioned: John 20:21-23

A. Jesus Sent Them: vs. 21

Again Jesus said, "Peace be with you! As the Father has sent me, I am sending you."

20:21 "As the Father has sent me, I am sending you."

This is essentially Jesus' "commissioning" of the disciples in the fourth Gospel, similar to Matthew. 28:19-20. Here both verbs for "sending" occur together in the same verse.

Having pronounced peace upon His friends, Jesus pointed them away from their despair toward the future. He had important things for them to do for the advancement of His kingdom. They had to overcome their fears of the Roman and Jewish rulers, and find a new mission in life.

Jesus did not describe their work in detail, but used a very clear, simple word—"send." A Latin version of this verb "to send" (missio) is the root of our word mission. He also gave them a clear pattern of what it would be like—His own mission from His Father.

On this occasion, Jesus did not tell them where His mission would take them, but it was the whole world (Matt. 28:19; Mark 16:15; Acts 1:8). This promise in the upper room was the foundation for the subsequent growth and expansion of the church. Ever since, the church has accepted it as a classic missionary text.

The heart of Christ's mission was self-giving for others. Jesus had relinquished heaven's glory for a time. He came in humility to seek and to save the lost. He came to do His Father's will (John 4:34). His obedience was painfully costly, and in the end it cost Him His life. That's how His disciples were to engage in His mission—with humble, self-giving obedience for the sake of others.

B. Jesus Promised the Holy Spirit: vs. 22

And with that he breathed on them and said, "Receive the Holy Spirit."

In the upper room with His disciples, before He went with them to Gethsemane, Jesus had explained that He was going to send the

Holy Spirit to them (John 14—16). Having accomplished His death and resurrection, Jesus simply told them to receive the Holy Spirit. They could not possibly carry out His work without the Holy Spirit's wisdom, protection, and power. That's why Jesus told them to wait in Jerusalem until the Holy Spirit fell upon them (Acts 1:4-8). Jesus gave His chosen disciples peace behind their locked door, and He gave them power. They would no longer be chained by fear.

The word for spirit is *pneuma,* meaning breath or spirit. Therefore, it was fitting that Jesus breathed on them, to give them the Holy Spirit in anticipation of Pentecost.

C. Jesus Gave Authority: vs. 23

"If you forgive anyone his sins, they are forgiven; if you do not forgive them, they are not forgiven."

Jesus also gave His followers spiritual authority for their mission. In this statement, Jesus revealed the heart of their work. It had to do with offering people forgiveness of sins. Christ's mission was not primarily physical release but spiritual deliverance. He shed His blood for the remission of sins (Matt. 28). He came to seek and save the lost (Luke 19:10). This was to be the Church's pattern from the beginning—bringing spiritual salvation to a lost and dying world. Of course, ultimately God alone forgives and condemns, depending on a person's response to the Good News. But with this remarkable delegation of ministerial authority, Jesus' followers could and did tell people they were forgiven. When people come to faith in Christ, and accept His death and resurrection for their sins, they may rightfully claim God's forgiveness (1 John 1:9), and with the authority of God's Word we can assure them of that.

III. The Case of Thomas: John 20:24-29

A. He Did Not Believe: vss. 24-25

Now Thomas (called Didymus), one of the Twelve, was not with the disciples when Jesus came. So the other disciples told him, "We have seen the Lord!" But he said to them, "Unless I see the nail marks in his hands and put my finger where the nails were, and put my hand into his side, I will not believe it."

Thomas missed the appearance of Jesus to His disciples in their hiding place. The writer does not tell us why he was absent, but the reason is not as important as what happened when he returned.

The dominating thought in the mind of the disciples was having seen the risen Jesus. We can hear them shouting the joyous news to Thomas. But their enthusiasm was squelched by Thomas's refusal to accept their testimony. "Really?" he seems to have said. He was unconvinced, so he demanded firsthand evidence of Christ's wounds suffered on the cross. Until he saw the wounds, he would not believe that Jesus had been raised from the dead.

Ever since he made those demands for evidence, Thomas has been labeled a doubter. The essence of doubt is to demand a peculiar and specific kind of proof, while disregarding evidence on other grounds. However, as the record shows, the other disciples also doubted Mary Magdalene's testimony, so perhaps it's unfair to single out Thomas for criticism.

Perhaps Thomas falls into the category of what we call "honest" doubters. His mind was still open to proof, and he chose to remain with the other disciples. They had accepted the fact that Jesus was alive, but this did not create a split in their ranks.

B. Jesus Appeared Again: vs. 26
A week later his disciples were in the house again, and Thomas was with them. Though the doors were locked, Jesus came and stood among them and said, "Peace be with you!"

Jesus did not give up on Thomas. Once more, He passed through the room's locked doors and greeted His disciples. The big difference was that Thomas was with them this time.

This was the sixth of Christ's 15 postresurrection appearances recorded in the Bible. This event occurred "a week later," that is, the Sunday following the day of His resurrection. Presumably, the disciples were still in hiding somewhere in Jerusalem.

C. Jesus Invited Thomas: vs. 27
Then he said to Thomas, "Put your finger here; see my hands. Reach out your hand and put it into my side. Stop doubting and believe."

Jesus picked up Thomas's challenge, point by point, and invited him to touch His hands and His side. Then He commanded him to surrender his doubts and believe. "Stop doubting" means "do not be faithless."

20:25 "I will not believe"

What Thomas was refusing to "believe" here was that Jesus had risen from the dead, as reported by his fellow disciples. The narrative's dramatic tension is heightened when Thomas, seeing for himself the risen Jesus, believes more than just the resurrection.

50

Jesus helped His unbelieving disciple come to faith. He did not reject Thomas because he had demanded proof that He had risen from the grave. This intensely personal encounter has encouraged many doubters. This story encourages sincere investigation of all the facts. Anyone who is serious about Christ's claims—His deity and resurrection—will find plenty of evidence to support them.

D. Thomas Confessed: vs. 28

Thomas said to him, "My Lord and my God!"

Apparently Thomas did not accept Jesus' offer to touch His body. When Thomas saw Jesus and heard His invitation to believe, he broke down and confessed his faith. He willingly gave himself to Christ without further reservations. He moved from being faithless to believing.

E. Jesus Encouraged Faith: vs. 29

Then Jesus told him, "Because you have seen me, you have believed; blessed are those who have not seen and yet have believed."

Jesus loved Thomas, gave him ample proof, and accepted his confession of personal faith. Thomas had the wonderful opportunity and advantage of seeing Jesus in person. He saw and believed.

But Jesus looked beyond Thomas to the future, when countless thousands of people would believe without benefit of physical evidence they could see with their eyes. Their faith rested on the eyewitness testimony of the disciples. That is why the Gospel records are so important. In effect, they are God's testimony about His Son (1 John 5:11). The church offers the evidence to people, so they can believe and be saved.

Discussion Questions

1. Why do you think the disciples were unprepared for Christ's resurrection?
2. How would you write the script for their conversation in their hiding place?
3. What fears do people have today about the future, and how can Christians help them with the good news of the risen Christ?
4. Is being commissioned by Jesus something reserved for full-time Christian workers, pastors, and missionaries? How could a plumber feel that he has been "sent" by Jesus?
5 What was Thomas's basic problem?
6. How does his story encourage people to be honest doubters?

Now Ask Yourself . . .

When I have doubts about God, how do I handle them?
Do I choose to believe even if there is no visual evidence?
Am I carrying out the great commission in my life today?

Illustrations

When the disciples saw Jesus, they were glad. When they told Thomas, he demanded to see for himself. When he saw Jesus, he confessed his faith. Jesus made sure that His team was absolutely convinced that He was alive and that He was Lord and God. Therefore, they were fit and armed to be sent into the unbelieving world.

The Lord's army cannot march on short rations. The day demands that the people of God be fully armed, intellectually, volitionally, and emotionally—mind, will, and heart. Doubters in the ranks destroy the army's effectiveness. Jesus demands our all, but emotional responses are insufficient. If our minds and wills are not totally His, no amount of enthusiasm will carry the day.

Therefore, the Church's task is to help people meet the risen Christ face-to-face, as it were. People who meet Him like Thomas did will be prepared for Christ's mission in the world. Without such a life-changing encounter, our involvement in this mission is doomed to futility and frustration.

The Promise of the Spirit's Power

Scripture
Background Scripture: *Acts 1*
Scripture Lesson: *Acts 1:3-14*
Key Verse: *"But you will receive power when the Holy Spirit comes on you; and you will be my witnesses in Jerusalem, and in all Judea and Samaria, and to the ends of the earth." Acts 1:8.*

Lesson Aim
To seek the Spirit's power to become better witnesses for Christ.

Lesson Setting
Time: A.D. 30
Place: Jerusalem and the Mount of Olives

Lesson Outline
The Promise of the Spirit's Power
  I. The Promise of the Spirit: Acts 1:3-8
      A. *The Savior's Postresurrection Appearances: vs. 3*
      B. *The Command to Wait: vss. 4-5*
      C. *The Disciples' Question about the Kingdom: vs. 6*
      D. *The Savior's Promise of the Spirit: vss. 7-8*
  II. The Ascension of the Savior: Acts 1:9-11
      A. *The Savior's Departure: vs. 9*
      B. *The Savior's Promised Return: vss. 10-11*
  III. The Disciples at Prayer: Acts 1:12-14

53

Introduction

*The Promise of
Empowerment*

Most adults in our society are self-sufficient and have great difficulty depending on others for help. In fact, it's our human nature to seek control over our circumstances and power over people. With children, this struggle for power is obvious in physical grabbing and pushing. As adults we become more subtle. We manipulate and play politics.

Not surprisingly, our tendency is to try to convert people to Christ on our own strength. This week's lesson, however, asks us to reconsider what is the true source of the power that enables us to witness and that brings people to Christ. Indeed, God claims that we are powerless to have any effectiveness without His help. Ultimately, it's His power that brings people to faith and transforms the way they think and act.

Lesson Commentary

I. The Promise of the Spirit: Acts 1:3-8

A. The Savior's Postresurrection Appearances: vs. 3

After his suffering, he showed himself to these men and gave many convincing proofs that he was alive. He appeared to them over a period of forty days and spoke about the kingdom of God.

Luke, the writer of the Gospel that bears his name, also penned its sequel, the Book of Acts. This document picks up the account where the Gospels leave off by telling about the early days of the Church. In fact, Acts bridges the gap between the Gospel narratives and the letters of instruction that comprise most of the rest of the New Testament.

The focus of Luke's first book was "all that Jesus began to do and to teach" (Acts 1:1). The word *began* implies that the works and teaching of Jesus continued after His earthly ministry. From Luke's perspective the actions of the apostles after the Resurrection and Ascension were an extension of the ministry of Jesus, carried on through the power of the Spirit.

Prior to Jesus' ascension, He appeared to the apostles on several occasions over a span of 40 days. Jesus had two purposes during this period. First, He wanted to convince His followers that He truly had risen from the dead in bodily form. Before Jesus' resurrection, His followers had argued with each other, deserted their Lord, and one (Peter) even lied about knowing Jesus. After the Resurrection, Jesus met with His apostles and answered their questions.

Christ also removed His followers' doubts through "many convincing proofs" (1:3). For instance, to give the apostles confidence to present His message, He entered a locked room (John 20:19), showed His crucifixion wounds (Luke 24:39), and ate and drank with the disciples (vss. 41-43).

Jesus' second purpose was to teach His followers about God's kingdom. "Kingdom" (Acts 1:3) translates *basileias* [bah-sih-LAY-us], from which we get our English word *basilica*. The term refers to the rule of God over His creation. The Kingdom embraces all who walk in fellowship with God and do His will.

B. The Command to Wait: vss. 4-5

On one occasion, while he was eating with them, he gave them this command: "Do not leave Jerusalem, but wait for the gift my Father promised, which you have heard me speak about. For John baptized with water, but in a few days you will be baptized with the Holy Spirit."

The Lord's teaching during this 40-day period included a command that the apostles were to wait in Jerusalem until they had received the gift of the Holy Spirit (Acts 1:4). At this point it's helpful to consider the nature of the Spirit's work among the people of God in the Old Testament era (namely, before the day of Pentecost).

While the Old Testament mentions the Spirit of God frequently, it tells little about people possessing the Spirit. The Old Testament does, however, reveal that those who experienced the Spirit in that era included rulers, such as elders (Num. 11:25), judges (Judg. 3:10), and kings (1 Sam. 16:13). Prophets also experienced the Spirit (Ezek. 2:2). In at least one case, an artisan experienced God's Spirit (Exod. 31:3). And the Spirit was sometimes withdrawn from people (1 Sam. 16:14).

Taking all the evidence into consideration, the impression conveyed is that the Spirit mainly came upon selected individuals for specific jobs in the Old Testament era. However, Old Testament prophets entertained a lively hope that a time was coming when

---

"The Spirit"

The coming of the Spirit would unite all the believers into one body, to be known as the church (1 Cor. 12:13). The Spirit would also give the believers power to witness to the lost. Finally, the Spirit would enable the believers to speak in tongues and perform other miraculous deeds to awaken the Jews.

God's Spirit would be given out more broadly (Isa. 32:15; 59:21; Joel 2:28-29). That hope was partially fulfilled on the day of Pentecost (John 14:16; Acts 2:14-21).

What was Jesus' purpose for having the disciples wait until the Spirit came? One reason may have been so that the fulfillment of the promise might coincide with the day of Pentecost and mark the beginning of a new phase in the development of God's plan. From a practical perspective the waiting period possibly impressed the disciples with the important role the Spirit would serve in the fulfillment of their mission. As important as that mission was, it could not begin until the Spirit had been given.

In Acts 1:5, Jesus drew a contrast between the baptism performed by John and that provided by the Spirit. The first was physical in nature ("with water") while the second was supernatural in nature ("with the Holy Spirit"). The passive tense of the Greek verb rendered "will be baptized" indicates that this act did not depend on the efforts of Jesus' followers to bring about, but rather on the work of the Lord. Through the ministry of the Spirit, the disciples would be placed into spiritual union with one another in the Body of Christ, the Church (1 Cor. 12:12-13).

C. The Disciples' Question about the Kingdom: vs. 6

So when they met together, they asked him, "Lord, are you at this time going to restore the kingdom to Israel?"

The disciples still struggled to understand God's plans. They thought the Jewish nation and the kingdom of God were practically synonymous. They couldn't imagine a higher purpose for the promised Messiah than to deliver the Jewish people from their hated Roman oppressors.

D. The Savior's Promise of the Spirit: vss. 7-8

He said to them: "It is not for you to know the times or dates the Father has set by his own authority. But you will receive power when the Holy Spirit comes on you; and you will be my witnesses in Jerusalem, and in all Judea and Samaria, and to the ends of the earth."

The disciples had framed their question in a way that expected an immediate fulfillment to God's plans. The fact that they spoke only of restoring the kingdom of Israel also indicates that their initial expectation was limited to the Jews. Jesus, however, had an objective that was worldwide in scope.

In response to the disciples' question, Jesus declared that the issue of timing was a matter reserved exclusively for God the Father. "Times" (Acts 1:7) refers to chronology or the duration of time (in other words, "how long"). "Dates" refers to the epochs or events that take place within time. The disciples were not to know how long it would be before Christ returned, nor were they to be preoccupied with the events preceding His second coming. Rather, they were to trust that all things would happen in God's time and in His way.

Rather than fixate upon the future, the disciples were to proclaim the Gospel throughout the world. Jesus knew that they could not do this on their own. They would need supernatural assistance. In fact, their success depended on the gift promised by the Father, namely, the Holy Spirit.

Jesus explained that when the Spirit came, the disciples would receive an infusion of supernatural "power" (Acts 1:8). They then would be filled with courage and ability to witness about Jesus. The Greek term rendered "witnesses" is the same one from which the word martyr is derived. It was originally a legal term used for those who gave evidence at a trial. Eventually the church came to view martyrs as those who died for their faith. In verse 8, however, the living testimony of the disciples is in view. In Acts, the term is used specifically of the disciples' role as ambassadors of the risen Christ (2:32; 3:15; 10:39-41).

Jesus described expanding zones of influence, beginning at Jerusalem, spreading throughout Judea and Samaria, and eventually reaching "the ends of the earth" (1:8). Commentators have noted that the movement of the Book of Acts itself follows this general pattern of expansion. In the first part, Luke detailed the witness of the church in Jerusalem (1:1—8:3). In the second part, he discussed the witness of the church in Judea and Samaria (8:4—12:24). And in the third part, Luke related the witness of the church to the farthest corners of the earth (12:25—28:31).

II. The Ascension of the Savior: Acts 1:9-11

A. The Savior's Departure: vs. 9

After he said this, he was taken up before their very eyes, and a cloud hid him from their sight.

The disciples watched as Jesus was taken up into heaven (Acts

1:9). Luke stressed the fact that they actually saw Jesus ascend until He disappeared from their sight. This was not a hallucination or a vision, but rather a real event.

The cloud that received Jesus reminds us of the cloud that was known as the Shekinah—the visible manifestation of God's glory and presence—in the Old Testament era. The cloud surrounding Jesus was a visible reminder that God's glory was present as the disciples watched the Savior's gradual, majestic departure from earth.

B. The Savior's Promised Return: vss. 10-11

They were looking intently up into the sky as he was going, when suddenly two men dressed in white stood beside them. "Men of Galilee," they said, "why do you stand here looking into the sky? This same Jesus, who has been taken from you into heaven, will come back in the same way you have seen him go into heaven."

The commissioning of the disciples was Jesus' last word to them before He ascended. As He disappeared from their sight, they suddenly must have felt all alone. But as if one remarkable sight wasn't enough for one day, the disciples next saw two angels in the appearance of men standing beside them. These angels reassured the disciples that Jesus was not gone forever. He would return in just the same way He had departed (Acts 1:10-11).

The promise of Jesus' return to earth should encourage us, as it undoubtedly did the disciples, to live faithfully for Him. We are not to be escapists—barely holding on, waiting for Christ to return and take us out of this world with its troubles. Christ's return, instead, should motivate us in our service and dedication to Him as Lord.

III. The Disciples at Prayer: Acts 1:12-14

Then they returned to Jerusalem from the hill called the Mount of Olives, a Sabbath day's walk from the city. When they arrived, they went upstairs to the room where they were staying. Those present were Peter, John, James and Andrew; Philip and Thomas, Bartholomew and Matthew; James son of Alphaeus and Simon the Zealot, and Judas son of James. They all joined together constantly in prayer, along with the women and Mary the mother of Jesus, and with his brothers.

After the Ascension, Jesus' disciples returned to Jerusalem, where they met in an upper room (Acts 1:12-13). The upper room of large homes was often rented out to the poor. It's possible that this was the same upper room where Jesus had celebrated His last Passover with the disciples.

Some think the upper room may have been in the house owned by Mary, the mother of John Mark, who was the author of the Gospel of Mark and a relative of Barnabas. This room served both as temporary lodging and a place of prayer for the early church.

Luke noted that all the apostles (with the exception of Judas Iscariot) and several of the women who had followed Jesus were gathered in the upper room for prayer (vs. 14). In addition, Luke mentioned Mary, the mother of Jesus, and His brothers. Apparently, the Savior's resurrection had convinced His brothers to put their faith in Him as the Messiah (John 7:5).

The disciples' prayer activity was characterized by a unity of thought and purpose. During this time, they may have praised Jesus for being the Messiah, thanked God for choosing them to be His servants, and asked for courage and the faith to remain devoted to Christ.

Discussion Questions

1. Why do you think Luke placed emphasis on the Holy Spirit as he began the Book of Acts?
2. What did it mean for the disciples to be witnesses for Jesus? What does it mean for us to be His witnesses?
3. Why was it important for the disciples to witness Jesus' ascension?
4. What is the role of the Spirit in the church today?
5. What evidence of the Spirit's power have you seen in your own life?
6. Why is it important to know that witnessing includes relying on the Spirit's power as well as communicating facts presented in the Gospel?

Now Ask Yourself . . .

Do I rely on my own power or the power of the Holy Spirit to obey and serve the Lord?

How is the Holy Spirit manifested in my daily life?

Illustrations

Jesus' plan for the Church was larger than any of the disciples could have imagined. It must have seemed incredible to this small group of approximately 120 people to hear that their efforts would eventually have a worldwide impact. Such a mission required nothing less than the power of God's own Spirit to ensure its fulfillment.

The emphasis on power in Jesus' promise to the Church contrasts with the weakness the disciples must have felt after Christ's death. Afraid of the authorities and ashamed of their own failure to stand with Jesus in His hour of humiliation, they must have wondered how they could possibly be effective witnesses to the ends of the earth.

This mission could be fulfilled only through God's strength. No amount of natural courage or human resolve could match the empowerment that would come from the outpouring of God's Spirit. The role played by the Spirit in the mission of the early church was so important that the disciples could not even begin to fulfill that assignment until they had received His enabling.

What does this mean for us, now that we have God's Spirit? The Third Person of the Trinity empowers us to be witnesses for Christ by providing us with spiritual discernment, courage, and love. The Spirit also changes our character and life so that we are more Christlike in what we say and do.

If we attempt to live our Christian life in our own limited strength, we can expect failure, disappointment, and frustration. On the other hand, if we depend on the power of the Spirit, God Himself will strengthen us to be like Christ and to tell others about Him. While there is some disagreement among believers regarding certain details of the Spirit's work, all agree that holy living and effective service are possible only through the Spirit's power.

The Holy Spirit Comes in Power

Scripture

Background Scripture: *Acts 2*

Scripture Lesson: *Acts 2:1-4, 37-47*

Key Verse: *All the believers were together and had everything in common. Acts 2:44*

Lesson Aim

To give evidence of the Spirit's presence by helping others in need.

Lesson Setting

Time: A.D. 30

Place: Jerusalem

Lesson Outline

The Holy Spirit Comes in Power

   I. The Spirit's Coming: Acts 2:1-4
     A. *Meeting Together: vs. 1*
     B. *Being Filled with the Spirit: vss. 2-4*
  II. The People's Response: Acts 2:37-42
     A. *The Question from the Audience: vs. 37*
     B. *The Response of Peter: vss. 38-40*
     C. *The Transformation of Many Lives: vss. 41-42*
 III. The Believers' Sharing: Acts 2:43-47
     A. *The Apostles' Miracles: vs. 43*
     B. *The Believers' Generosity: vss. 44-45*
     C. *The Believers' Worship and Praise: vss. 46-47*

Introduction

Empowered By the Spirit

Riding through a town, a young man observed a sign on a church that read "Jesus Saves!" The man commented, "I didn't know that Jesus taught us to be thrifty!"

Such a flippant remark suggests that the question "Are you saved?" has little meaning for most people today. It's no wonder we have backed off from asking the lost this question. It's sad, for on the day of Pentecost being saved was a crucial issue for Jesus' followers. Consider Peter. The Spirit empowered him to preach a moving sermon about salvation, and many people responded by repenting of their sins and trusting in Christ.

We don't have to be tactless in asking whether an acquaintance is saved. Of course, we may have to explain what we mean to those who have little, if any, understanding of spiritual matters. Though our efforts may seem feeble, they're not. We can trust the Spirit to give us courage and wisdom, especially as we urge unbelievers to be saved from their sins.

Lesson Commentary

I. The Spirit's Coming: Acts 2:1-4

A. Meeting Together: vs. 1

When the day of Pentecost came, they were all together in one place.

The events of this week's lesson took place one to two weeks after Jesus' ascension into heaven, on the "day of Pentecost" (Acts 2:1). The name Pentecost comes from a Greek word meaning "fiftieth." The festival fell on the fiftieth day after the Passover Sabbath.

Along with the festivals of unleavened bread and tabernacles, Pentecost was one of the three great Jewish religious holy days. The population of Jerusalem swelled during each of these festivals as pilgrims streamed into the city from all over.

The risen Lord had commanded His disciples not to immediately leave Jerusalem but to wait for the arrival of the Spirit (Luke 24:49; Acts 1:4). In obedience to Jesus, His disciples were "all together in one place" (Acts 2:1). Two truths are evident from this statement. First, the disciples were assembled in one location. Second, they were in agreement in their thinking and purpose.

B. Being Filled with the Spirit: vss. 2-4

Suddenly a sound like the blowing of a violent wind came from heaven and filled the whole house where they were sitting. They saw what seemed to be tongues of fire that separated and came to rest on each of them. All of them were filled with the Holy Spirit and began to speak in other tongues as the Spirit enabled them.

Suddenly and unexpectedly the disciples heard a sound from heaven that was similar to that of a turbulent wind. The noise filled the "whole house" (Acts 2:2) they were in. Some think Christ's followers were at that moment in one of the courts of the Jerusalem temple (Luke 24:52-53), while others maintain that the disciples were in the upper room of a house (Acts 1:13).

In the context of this incident, the wind was a physical indication of the presence of the Spirit. In Scripture wind and breath are common symbols of God's Spirit (Ezek. 37:9, 14; John 3:8).

The sight of "tongues of fire that separated" (Acts 2:3) was even more unusual than the sound of the wind. These tongue-shaped flames appeared to stand over each disciple's head. This incident was significant because it indicated that God's presence was among His followers. Thus the disciples could sense the Spirit's coming audibly (through wind) and visibly (through fire).

In fact, the disciples "were filled with the Holy Spirit" (vs. 4). As evidence of His presence, the Spirit enabled them to "speak in other tongues." Apparently these supernatural "tongues" were actual languages or dialects being spoken by the disciples to the various visitors from many countries in Jerusalem. The Spirit had come to empower Jesus' followers to reach out to the lost with the saving message of the Gospel.

Some in the crowd were genuinely amazed at what had happened, while others mockingly accused Jesus' followers of being drunk (vss. 12-13). At this point, Peter stood up and addressed the crowd. He first made it clear that Jesus' followers were not drunk (vss. 14-15). Then, after interpreting the foreign tongues as fulfillment of Scripture (vss. 16-21), Peter began to speak about Jesus' resurrection (vss. 22-24).

Peter next quoted from Psalm 16:8-11 (Acts 2:25-28). He then reassured his audience that this portion of Scripture, though written by the patriarch David under the Spirit's inspiration, did not fully apply to David because he had died and was buried. In fact, David's corpse still lay in his royal tomb in Jerusalem, which the

"Tongues"

The believers spoke in tongues. They did not preach in tongues, but rather praised God in languages they did not naturally know (2:11). Apparently they were in the Upper Room when the Spirit descended, but must have moved out to the temple courts where a great crowd gathered. The purpose of the gift of tongues was to impress the Jews with the fact that a miracle was taking place. In 10:46, the Gentiles spoke with tongues as proof to the apostles that they had received the Spirit; and in 19:6 the Ephesian followers of John the Baptist spoke in tongues for the same reason.

people in the crowd could visit (vs. 29).

Peter revealed that David had spoken as a prophet regarding the Messiah. God had promised David that Christ would be his descendant. David understood not only that the Messiah would be raised from the dead but also that He would reign as King (vss. 30-31). Peter said that he and the rest of the disciples had witnessed Jesus' bodily resurrection (vs. 32). Though some in the crowd probably disputed Peter's statement about Jesus' resurrection, Peter and the rest of the disciples were willing to courageously testify to the truth (vss. 33-36).

As we study Acts, we will see the theme of Christ's resurrection turning up again and again in the life and message of the early church. It became the loom that held the fabric of the Gospel together. Without the Resurrection, there would have been nothing to say.

Jesus' resurrection must remain central to our faith. We cannot reserve it for a seasonal emphasis at Easter and still have the vibrancy of faith that the apostles had. Christ's resurrection should be the foundation for everything we build as a church.

II. The People's Response: Acts 2:37-42

A. The Question from the Audience: vs. 37

When the people heard this, they were cut to the heart and said to Peter and the other apostles, "Brothers, what shall we do?"

In Acts 2:36, Peter declared, "God has made this Jesus, whom you crucified, both Lord and Christ." Upon hearing this, the crowd was "cut to the heart" (vs. 37), which means they were remorseful. Genuinely grieving over their rejection of the Messiah, they asked Peter and the rest of the apostles what was necessary for them to get right with God.

The audience responded this way to Peter because he had communicated the Gospel with power and courage. More importantly, Peter's message convicted his hearers of sin and then spoke of God's mercy and love.

B. The Response of Peter: vss. 38-40

Peter replied, "Repent and be baptized, every one of you, in the name of Jesus Christ for the forgiveness of your sins. And you will receive the gift of the Holy Spirit. The promise is for you and your children and for all who are far off—for all whom the Lord our God will call." With many other words he warned them; and he pleaded with them, "Save yourselves from this corrupt generation."

Peter told his audience to repent and be baptized "in the name of Jesus Christ" (Acts 2:38). Some have noted that the baptismal formula in this verse is shorter than the one appearing in Matthew 28:19. Based on this difference, it is suggested that at least two different versions were used in the early church.

Others think the shorter version complemented the fuller one. According to this view, the shorter formula was used to underscore the new relationship between Christ and believers, while the longer formula emphasized their intimate union with all three persons of the Godhead.

Baptism would publicly announce the audience's new relationship as believers in Jesus. In Bible times religious rites involving water were commonplace. For example, baptism was a requirement for Gentile proselytes to Judaism. This was their way of openly identifying themselves with the God of Israel, His laws, and His people.

By trusting in Jesus the Messiah for salvation, the people would be forgiven of all their transgressions and experience God's mercy. Peter assured his listeners they would "receive the gift of the Holy Spirit" (Acts 2:38). God's promise of the Spirit was not meant just for those listening to Peter. It was also intended for their descendants and people in distant places who would receive Christ (vss. 39-40).

C. The Transformation of Many Lives: vss. 41-42

Those who accepted his message were baptized, and about three thousand were added to their number that day. They devoted themselves to the apostles' teaching and to the fellowship, to the breaking of bread and to prayer.

Pentecost was a strategic time for God to send the Holy Spirit. Pilgrims who heard God being praised in their own languages were among that day's 3,000 converts (Acts 2:41). God would use them to take the good news of salvation in Christ back with them to their homelands.

The Holy Spirit gave profound unity and joy to the early believers. The large group listened to the apostles' teaching. They gave themselves to fellowshipping with one another. They remembered Christ's death through the celebration of the Lord's Supper. And they spent hours in prayer, praising God and interceding for one another (vs. 42).

Praying is talking to God. The act of praying does not change what God has purposed to do. Rather, it is the means by which He accomplishes His will. Talking to God is not a method of creating a positive mental attitude in ourselves so that we are able to do what we want to be done. Instead, prayer creates within us a right attitude with respect to the will of God. Prayer is not so much getting God to do our will as it is demonstrating that we are as concerned as He is that His will be done (Matt. 6:10).

III. The Believers' Sharing: Acts 2:43-47

A. The Apostles' Miracles: vs. 43

Everyone was filled with awe, and many wonders and miraculous signs were done by the apostles.

The Spirit gave further vindication of the Pentecost events by empowering the apostles to perform signs and wonders (Acts 2:43). They didn't regard these miracles as an end in itself. Rather, the works of power were done in the name of Christ and for His glory. The signs and wonders were intended to point people to Jesus and the truth of God's saving power through faith in Him.

B. The Believers' Generosity: vss. 44-45

All the believers were together and had everything in common. Selling their possessions and goods, they gave to anyone as he had need.

All those who had trusted in Christ not only stayed together but also shared their belongings with one another (Acts 2:44). In fact, God's people were willing to sell "their possessions and goods" (vs. 45). The mutual generosity of the believers ensured that those who were in need of essentials had those needs fully met.

Jesus' followers recognized that one of their responsibilities was to help people in whatever way possible. By doing this, they gave evidence of the Spirit's presence in their lives and showed that He had transformed them from selfish individuals into members of a caring community.

A key test of our commitment to Christ is our love for other believers (John 13:34). Such compassion is not a dry doctrine we affirm or a vague intellectual abstraction. Rather, God calls us to show love in concrete, relevant ways (1 John 3:16-18). It's not just our words that express our concern for others, but our attitudes and actions as well. Jesus did not say that others would know we are His disciples by what we say, how we dress, or what we know. Rather, it would be through our unselfish, unconditional love (John 13:35).

C. The Believers' Worship and Praise: vss. 46-47

Every day they continued to meet together in the temple courts. They broke bread in their homes and ate together with glad and sincere hearts, praising God and enjoying the favor of all the people. And the Lord added to their number daily those who were being saved.

The new converts to the faith had no meeting place of their own, so they gathered every day in the temple courts. They also met in their homes to share meals and observe the Lord's Supper. Their days were marked by genuine joy and sincerity. They encouraged one another, witnessed to the unsaved about Jesus, and worshiped the Lord (Acts 2:46).

Verse 47 says that the disciples were "praising God and enjoying the favor of all the people." The English word "praise" comes from a Latin verb that means "to value" or "to price." (Note its kinship with "appraise.") Thus, to give praise to God is to proclaim His merit or worth.

Praise is an act of worship in which we acknowledge the virtues and deeds of someone else. Often one human praising another, while sometimes commendable (1 Cor. 11:2), can become a snare (Prov. 27:21). In contrast, the praise we give to God honors Him and uplifts our souls (1 Chron. 29:13).

"Meet Together"

Note that the believers remained in the temple and gave their witness and worship. The Spirit gave them unity of heart and mind and added believers to the assembly day by day. These verses are a beautiful description of what life will be like during the kingdom age.

Discussion Questions

1. Why was it important for the disciples to be united in thought and purpose?
2. Why did the Spirit show Himself to the disciples both audibly and visibly?
3. Why was Christ's resurrection central to Peter's sermon?
4. Why do you think the early believers felt it was important to share what they owned with one another?
5. How can we be sure that the Spirit is present in our lives?
6. How does God's Spirit help you become more sensitive to the needs of others?

Now Ask Yourself . . .

What are my priorities?

Do I value God's power so that I may be a blessing to others? Or, do I only seek the power of God to make my life better?

Illustrations

Luke's description of life in the early church appears to be so idyllic that we think it's impossible to reproduce today. Wouldn't it be wonderful, we say, if thousands were saved every day? Wouldn't it be great if we shared our possessions, prayed together, and worshiped and witnessed in unity?

Of course, our immediate response would be yes, but then we confess that such things just don't happen that way in our churches. We admit defeat without really looking at the reasons for what happened on Pentecost. It's true that some aspects of that time period were unique; nevertheless, the principles evident from the way in which God worked haven't changed.

For instance, the Holy Spirit dwells in God's people and enables them to tell others about Christ's death and resurrection. The Lord calls believers to unity, generosity, prayer, and worship. When they confess their need for spiritual power, God answers.

Perhaps our problem is that we don't desire these things as much as we say we do. Perhaps we have higher priorities and goals for ourselves and our churches. It's only when we put Jesus and His people first in our lives that we will see the Lord adding to our congregations "those who [are] being saved" (Acts 2:47).

The Holy Spirit Works with Power

Scripture

Background Scripture: *Acts 3:1—4:13*
Scripture Lesson: *Acts 3:1-10; 4:1-4, 13*
Key Verse: *When they saw the courage of Peter and John and realized that they were unschooled, ordinary men, they were astonished and they took note that these men had been with Jesus. Acts 4:13*

Lesson Aim

To rejoice in the life-changing power of Jesus Christ.

Lesson Setting

Time: A.D. 30
Place: Jerusalem

Lesson Outline

The Holy Spirit Works with Power

I. The Healing at the Temple: Acts 3:1-10
  A. *The Request of the Cripple: vss. 1-3*
  B. *The Healing of the Cripple: vss. 4-8*
  C. *The Response of the Crowd: vss. 9-10*
II. The Arrest of Peter and John: Acts 4:1-4, 13
  A. *The Agitation of the Religious Leaders: vss. 1-3*
  B. *The Conversion of Many People: vs. 4*
  C. *The Bewilderment of the Religious Leaders:*
    vs. 13

Introduction

Empowered for Service

Evangelism is a word that scares many Christians. We think telling others about Christ is the responsibility of religious experts. But this week's lesson reminds us that untrained believers made a significant impact for Christ in the first century A.D. It was possible because they operated in the life-changing power of Christ.

God gives us many opportunities to point others to Jesus. When we meet people at their deepest physical and social needs, for example, we gain opportunities to share that we serve in the name and power of Christ.

Perhaps we fail to see beyond the outward appearance of many people. We think they don't need religious faith. But as we get to know them, they often admit to some glaring spiritual needs. As one woman told her friends, "The best Christmas gift I can give my family is to get my spiritual life straightened out." She has since that time come to faith in Christ!

Lesson Commentary

I. The Healing at the Temple: Acts 3:1-10

A. The Request of the Cripple: vss. 1-3

One day Peter and John were going up to the temple at the time of prayer—at three in the afternoon. Now a man crippled from birth was being carried to the temple gate called Beautiful, where he was put every day to beg from those going into the temple courts. When he saw Peter and John about to enter, he asked them for money.

In the weeks following Pentecost, the apostles performed "miracles, wonders and signs" (Acts 2:22) as proof that the risen Christ changes lives. Luke provided a specific example in the case of a disabled beggar who sought alms at the Beautiful Gate of the temple in Jerusalem (3:2).

The Beautiful Gate was an entrance to the temple, not the city. It is usually thought to be the Gate of Nicanor, which was constructed of fine Corinthian brass and was adorned with much richer and thicker plates of silver and gold than the other gates. Some scholars think that it was from this silver and gold-plated gate that

Peter got the idea for his remark "Silver or gold I do not have" (vs. 6).

Persons with physical disabilities frequently came to the temple area to seek financial help. Since giving alms was regarded as particularly meritorious, beggars were likely to assemble where pious Jews might be counted on for generosity. The contrast between the richly ornamented Beautiful Gate and the beggar in rags must have been a striking one.

During the first century A.D., the Jews observed three daily periods of prayer—morning (9:00 a.m.), afternoon (3:00 p.m.), and evening (sunset). At these times Jews and devout Gentiles who believed in God went to the temple to pray. Peter and John were going there for the afternoon service when they noticed the beggar and heard his pleas for alms (vss. 1, 3).

This beggar had been crippled from birth, and he was now over 40 years old (3:2; 4:22). His disability was so severe that he had to be carried to the temple gate. There he begged each day for a handout from the temple worshipers.

In societies with no governmental welfare programs or social security, the unemployed and disabled usually had to resort to begging. The frequent mention of beggars in the New Testament suggests that they were a common sight on the city streets of Palestine.

B. The Healing of the Cripple: vss. 4-8

Peter looked straight at him, as did John. Then Peter said, "Look at us!" So the man gave them his attention, expecting to get something from them. Then Peter said, "Silver or gold I do not have, but what I have I give you. In the name of Jesus Christ of Nazareth, walk." Taking him by the right hand, he helped him up, and instantly the man's feet and ankles became strong. He jumped to his feet and began to walk. Then he went with them into the temple courts, walking and jumping, and praising God.

It's hard to imagine how the crippled man could have missed Jesus during the Lord's frequent visits to the temple. Since the beggar sat at one of the more heavily used entrances, he must have seen Jesus pass by on more than one occasion. Perhaps with the crowds and confusion that often accompanied Jesus, the man had not been able to get to the Savior for healing.

Another possibility is that God may have reserved this miracle of healing until after Jesus had ascended. By being done later, this work of power certified the ministry of the disciples and provided a major help for the young church.

By 3:00 p.m., when Peter and John arrived at the temple, the beggar may already have been at his post by the gate for most of the day. When he saw the two apostles, he gave out his usual call for help (Acts 3:3). However, he took no special notice of Peter and John, for most people passed by without giving anything.

The two apostles looked intently at the beggar (vs. 4). It was only when Peter called to him that he gave the two his full attention. Now the beggar was "expecting to get something from them" (vs. 5).

Peter declared that he had no funds to give, but that he had something else much better. Then, with the authority in Jesus' name, Peter commanded the disabled man to do what was physically impossible—to rise up and walk (vs. 6). The apostles were not interested in gaining attention or a following for themselves. They had only one priority—to accomplish the work Jesus had given them to do. They wanted to proclaim the good news about Christ everywhere they could to everyone they could.

At that moment a miracle occurred. As Peter lifted the beggar, he who had never learned to stand, let alone walk and leap, was on his feet, moving about freely and praising God. The man was filled with joy as he accompanied the apostles inside the temple courts (vss. 7-8).

C. The Response of the Crowd: vss. 9-10

When all the people saw him walking and praising God, they recognized him as the same man who used to sit begging at the temple gate called Beautiful, and they were filled with wonder and amazement at what had happened to him.

The people in the temple courts couldn't believe their eyes. They recognized the beggar easily enough. For years they had noticed him sitting in a heap before they could turn their gaze away from him. But now not only was he standing up, he wouldn't stop leaping about. Acts 3:9-10 suggest that the greatest miracle the man experienced on that day was not the healing of his legs but rather the salvation of his sin-sick soul. The church got a new member that day!

"Crippled"

This cripple is a vivid illustration of the lost sinner in that: (1) he was born lame, and all are born sinners; (2) he could not walk, and no sinner can walk so as to please God; (3) he was outside the temple, and sinners are outside God's temple, the church; (4) he was begging, for sinners are beggars, searching for satisfaction.

II. The Arrest of Peter and John: Acts 4:1-4, 13

A. The Agitation of the Religious Leaders: vss. 1-3

The priests and the captain of the temple guard and the Sadducees came up to Peter and John while they were speaking to the people. They were greatly disturbed because the apostles were teaching the people and proclaiming in Jesus the resurrection of the dead. They seized Peter and John, and because it was evening, they put them in jail until the next day.

God often preceded the outreach of the early church with miracles. Signs and wonders could gather a crowd even without the advantages of mass media advertising. The Lord's power, coupled with biblical preaching, convinced people of the truth of the Gospel.

Peter and John, along with the healed beggar, moved out to the larger court of the Gentiles, and took up a position in a covered colonnade with one side open to the court. There a crowd quickly gathered to see if the fast-spreading rumor of a miracle was true.

An opportunity to preach to a crowd was just the thing Peter wanted. He began by noting that he had not made the crippled man walk; rather, Jesus had done it. This was the same person the authorities had rejected and executed. Peter boldly asserted, "You killed the author of life, but God raised him from the dead" (Acts 3:15).

As Peter continued to preach to the crowd in the temple, he told them that since the Messiah had come in fulfillment of prophecy, they should repent of their sins. By so doing, they would receive God's blessings and show they valued what God had revealed about the Messiah in the Old Testament.

As news spread of the miraculous healing of the disabled man in the temple area, the Jewish authorities confronted the apostles. Among them were the leading priests, the captain of the temple guard, and some of the Sadducees (4:1).

Perhaps the chain of events took place as follows. Several priests serving their allotted week's temple service (Luke 1:8, 23) were near Solomon's Colonnade and could hear Peter's declarations about Jesus the Messiah. Alarmed by what they considered dangerous teaching against Jewish authority, the priests probably alerted the commander of the temple police force. (He was a member of

---

The "Sadducees"

The Sadducees did not believe in the resurrection of the dead and were opposed to Peter's preaching. The priests, of course, did not want to be indicted for the crucifixion of Christ. Little did Israel's religious leaders realize that Peter's message was the one thing that could save their nation!

Had they admitted their sin and received Christ, He would have bestowed the promises that the prophets had proclaimed centuries before.

one of the important priestly families.) The priests also alerted the Sadducees, who held prominent positions in the Sanhedrin, the Jewish council.

The authorities—especially the Sadducees—were upset for two reasons. First, they were skeptics who rejected all the Old Testament except the books of Moses, and who denied the resurrection from the dead (Acts 23:8). Peter's teaching about the Resurrection challenged their beliefs (4:2).

Second, the religious leaders came from wealthy families and consorted with the Roman government in order to maintain their position, influence, and wealth. Rome was merciless against public disorders, and the Jewish authorities worried that if the apostles went unchecked, civil unrest would follow.

The last thing the religious leaders wanted was for a couple of Jewish men to declare the resurrection of a king. Thus in an attempt to protect the status quo, the authorities had Peter and John arrested. Since trials at night were illegal, the apostles were kept overnight before being brought before the Sanhedrin, or Jewish supreme court (vs. 3).

B. The Conversion of Many People: vs. 4

But many who heard the message believed, and the number of men grew to about five thousand.

Whatever the religious leaders hoped to accomplish, their strategy was foiled because many people in the crowd who had heard Peter put their faith in Jesus as the Messiah. Though God's servants were imprisoned, His saving message was not hindered (2 Tim. 2:9). The result of the authorities taking two disciples into custody was that the number of believers totaled about 5,000 men, not counting women and children (Acts 4:4).

C. The Bewilderment of the Religious Leaders: vs. 13

When they saw the courage of Peter and John and realized that they were unschooled, ordinary men, they were astonished and they took note that these men had been with Jesus.

The following day a cadre of religious leaders—"the rulers, elders and teachers of the law" (Acts 4:5)—met in Jerusalem. They were members of the Jewish high council, the same council that had condemned Jesus to death (Luke 22:66). It had 70 members plus the current high priest, who presided over the group. The Sadducees held a majority in this ruling group. These were wealthy, intellectual, and powerful men of Jerusalem.

After some guards had brought Peter and John into the chamber, the two were asked, "By what power or what name did you do this?" (Acts 4:7). Peter, under the guidance and power of the Spirit, zeroed in on the real issue, namely, the miracle that had recently taken place in the temple. The apostle declared that the crippled beggar was healed "by the name of Jesus Christ of Nazareth" (vs. 10).

Though Peter and John were supposed to be defendants at the proceedings, it appears that they actually put the Council on trial. Peter stated that the authorities were guilty of bringing about Jesus' crucifixion. But despite their evil intent, God raised Him from the dead. Peter then declared that there was no other name for people to call on for salvation (vs. 12).

The Council was astounded at the change in Peter and John. Their boldness was especially impressive since they had no formal training in the approved Jewish schools. The religious leaders also recognized that the two "had been with Jesus" (vs. 13). Fearing mob action, the Council released Peter and John, warning them not to speak or teach in Jesus' name (vss. 14-22).

It was God's Spirit who gave Peter and John the courage and words to speak before the religious leaders. In fact, the empowerment of the Spirit was a fulfillment of Jesus' promise prior to His ascension that the Spirit would give His disciples the power to witness for Him in Jerusalem (1:8).

Discussion Questions

1. Why was what Peter gave the disabled man better than what he first expected from Peter?
2. What role do you think faith played in the healing of the lame man?
3. Why were the members of the Council concerned about the apostles' authorization to heal?
4. What transformed the apostles into courageous witnesses for Christ?
5. In what ways do you rejoice at how God has changed you?
6. What testimonies about changed lives have strengthened your faith in Christ's resurrection power?

Now Ask Yourself . . .

How has my life been changed by the power of the Holy Spirit?

Am I willing to share with others how God's Spirit has delivered me from sins and transformed my life?

Illustrations

One of the clearest evidences of the Spirit's work was the change in the disciples after the resurrection of Jesus. Consider Peter. Because of his denial of Jesus before His crucifixion, we would hardly expect Peter to witness boldly in Jerusalem for the Savior. Yet when challenged by the authorities, Peter unflinchingly stood tall for Christ.

In addition to being courageous, the apostles resisted the temptation to take credit for the miraculous healing of the crippled man. Instead, Peter and John focused the people's attention on Christ. By invoking the name of Jesus, the apostles released the Savior's power to heal the beggar (Acts 3:6). And by faith in that name, the beggar received the power to stand up and walk (vs. 16).

The Spirit's power still changes lives. At times the power is evident in health situations where medical science has no explanation for the apparent healing. The Spirit's power also brings changes in behavior, turning around those who once lived selfishly, so that their lives now focus on others.

Although many worldly forces are intent on removing Christ from people's lives, they are feeble when they encounter the Savior's power. Thus we can rejoice, not only because His power is far greater than any earthly power, but also because His power has changed us.

Witnessing Beyond Jerusalem

Scripture

Background Scripture: *Acts 8:4-40*
Scripture Lesson: *Acts 8:4-8, 26-35*
Key Verse: *Those who had been scattered preached the word wherever they went. Acts 8:4*

Lesson Aim

To find ways to reach beyond social barriers with the good news of who Jesus is and what He has done.

Lesson Setting

Time: Around A.D. 34
Place: Samaria and the desert road going from Jerusalem to Gaza

Lesson Outline

Witnessing beyond Jerusalem

   I. Philip in Samaria: Acts 8:4-8
      A. The Spread of the Gospel: vs. 4
      B. The Ministry of Philip among the Samaritans: ....
      vss. 5-8
  II. Philip and the Ethiopian: Acts 8:26-35
      A. The Command of the Angel: vs. 26
      B. The Activities of the Ethiopian Eunuch:
      vss. 27-28
      C. The Question Asked by Philip: vss. 29-31
      D. The Scripture Passage Being Read by the
      Eunuch: vss. 32-33
      E. The Explanation Offered by Philip: vss. 34-35

Introduction

Called to Witness to All People

Promise Keepers is a Christian organization that has attracted tens of thousands of men of all races. One of the things this organization has attempted to do is break down the racial barriers that divide the church.

Social barriers come in many other forms besides racial: economic, academic, and gender (to name a few). Like most people, many of your students probably come to class with biases and social barriers that they may have never realized they have.

Some adults in your class may state, "It wasn't my fault, so I don't have to make the first gesture." If, however, we are to break down social barriers and proclaim the Gospel to other people, your students need to see what biases they have and be willing to make the first gesture.

Lesson Commentary

I. Philip in Samaria: Acts 8:4-8

A. The Spread of the Gospel: vs. 4

Those who had been scattered preached the word wherever they went.

After the death of Stephen (the first recorded Christian martyr), persecution broke out against the church. For fear of their lives, many disciples left Jerusalem and went into Judea and Samaria (Acts 8:1). Some understand this mass exodus from Jerusalem as also being the first missionary expedition of the church (8:4). Historically speaking, persecution has often had the opposite effect of those who perpetuate it.

God used persecution to spread the message of Jesus not only farther but also more rapidly (11:19). This fulfilled the second part of 1:8, where Jesus said the Gospel would spread from Jerusalem to Judea and Samaria and then to the ends of the earth.

B. The Ministry of Philip Among the Samaritans: vss. 5-8

Philip went down to a city in Samaria and proclaimed the Christ there. When the crowds heard Philip and saw the miraculous signs he did, they all paid close attention to what he said. With shrieks, evil spirits came out of many, and many paralytics and cripples were healed. So there was great joy in that city.

Philip was one of the seven believers in the Jerusalem church who had helped in the daily distribution of food (Acts 6:5). He was also among those who later left Jerusalem and proclaimed the Gospel to the unsaved. He traveled to Samaria and "proclaimed Christ there" (8:5).

It's unclear whether this city was the capital of Samaria or some other town in the area. In any case, it was common knowledge that Jews and Samaritans initiated no dealings with each other (John 4:9). For the most part, Jews saw Samaritans as ceremonially unclean half-breeds and religious deviants because they were descendants of Israelites who had intermarried with non-Israelites (2 Kings 17:24-41). Philip's commitment to Christ, however, enabled him to overcome any prejudice he might have had and preach the Gospel to the Samaritans.

Signs and wonders were the visible evidence that God was with Philip. When the people saw these works of power, they "all paid close attention to what he said" (Acts 8:6). The crowds marveled at the signs that Philip performed, and these served to confirm the truth of the Gospel. The supernatural acts, along with the preached word, brought deliverance and joy, the city (vss. 7-8).

The power of the Gospel to break down social barriers is seen in Philip's effective evangelism among the Samaritans. The miracles performed through him also showed the Samaritans that God's loved extended to all people who worship and serve Him. This truth is essential for anyone who seeks to bring others to Christ.

"Philip"

Philip was obedient to the Spirit, going where God led him. He knew Christ as his own Savior. God's method for winning others does not use organizational machinery, worldly attractions, or high-powered promotion. God uses people— dedicated men and women who will obey the Spirit. Philip was the kind of evangelist who was willing to leave the public meeting with its excitement to help a soul find peace in a private place where only God could see.

II. Philip and the Ethiopian: Acts 8:26-35

A. The Command of the Angel: vs. 26

Now an angel of the Lord said to Philip, "Go south to the road— the desert road—that goes down from Jerusalem to Gaza."

Simon, one who had formerly practiced sorcery and who had heard Philip preach the Gospel, believed and was baptized. The Jerusalem congregation dispatched Peter and John to Samaria, and God used them to impart the Spirit on the new converts. When Simon tried to purchase from Peter the power to impart the Spirit, the apostle rebuked him and urged him to repent of his wickedness. Through the ministry of Peter and John many more Samaritans heard the Gospel (Acts 8:9-25).

After revival had begun in Samaria, the angel of the Lord told Philip to leave the city and go south to the road that led from Jerusalem to Gaza (8:26). In ancient times this was a town located about 50 miles from Jerusalem. The original city was destroyed in the first century B.C. and a new city was built near the coast.

B. The Activities of the Ethiopian Eunuch: vss. 27-28

So he started out, and on his way he met an Ethiopian eunuch, an important official in charge of all the treasury of Candace, queen of the Ethiopians. This man had gone to Jerusalem to worship, and on his way home was sitting in his chariot reading the book of Isaiah the prophet.

On his way down the road, Philip met an Ethiopian eunuch (Acts 8:27). "Eunuch" refers either to an emasculated official in the royal court or to a high official of government. The Ethiopia (Cush) mentioned in Scripture was in the area south of Egypt and included parts of modern Eritrea, Ethiopia, and Sudan.

This Ethiopian (or Nubian) official was "in charge of all the treasury of Candace." "Candace" was the title of a succession of queen mothers who ruled. As the official treasurer to the queen, the eunuch was in charge of the financial affairs of the Nubian nation.

The presence of eunuchs from Africa and other places was common during this time. However, Philip's conversation with the Ethiopian official shows the inclusiveness of the Gospel. God's salvation through Christ is for persons of every race, kindred, and nation. In addition, Luke made it clear that God had arranged for this meeting not only to expand the spread of the Gospel but also to bring salvation to someone He loved.

The Ethiopian official had come to Jerusalem to attend a religious festival and was now on his way back to his native land. As he rode in his chariot, he read aloud to himself (vs. 28). Reading

aloud was a common practice in those days for those who had reading materials. But scrolls and other reading materials (which were
transcribed by hand) were not readily available to the average person. Only the wealthy and influential could afford literature. Even
more rare was a non-Jew possessing Hebrew Scripture, as this man
did.

Because the Ethiopian had managed to obtain a copy of Isaiah,
and since he had traveled to worship at the temple in Jerusalem, he
either was a convert to the Jewish faith or a "God-fearer." This label
referred to Gentiles who worshiped the true God but who had not
been circumcised.

C. The Question Asked by Philip: vss. 29-31

*The Spirit told Philip, "Go to that chariot and stay near it." Then
Philip ran up to the chariot and heard the man reading Isaiah the
prophet. "Do you understand what you are reading?" Philip asked.
"How can I," he said, "unless someone explains it to me?" So he
invited Philip to come up and sit with him.*

Philip sensed the Holy Spirit urging him closer to the chariot
(Acts 8:29). Philip promptly obeyed by running up to the
Ethiopian. Since the official was reading aloud, Philip evidently
knew the Scripture verses the eunuch was contemplating.
Knowing that this passage referred to the Suffering Servant, Philip
asked the Ethiopian if he understood what he was reading (vs. 30).

The official did not try to hide his ignorance. As one who
wanted to comprehend God's Word, he admitted that he needed
someone to explain the prophet's words. Perceiving that Philip was
such a person, the Ethiopian invited Philip to sit next to him in
his chariot.

D. The Scripture Passage Being Read by the Eunuch: vss. 32-33

*The eunuch was reading this passage of Scripture: "He was led like
a sheep to the slaughter, and as a lamb before the shearer is silent,
so he did not open his mouth. In his humiliation he was deprived
of justice. Who can speak of his descendants? For his life was taken
from the earth."*

The Ethiopian had been mulling over Isaiah 53:7 and 8. This
passage describes a person who submitted to affliction and death
without objection. He would do so to atone for human sin. He was

willing to die for others because He loved sinners and wanted to remove their transgressions.

By oppression and unjust judgment, this person would be taken away to His death. "And who can speak of his descendants?" Isaiah asked. The Jews believed that to die without children was a tragedy (2 Sam. 18:18). The suffering Servant would have no physical descendants, for He would be "cut off from the land of the living" (Isa. 53:8). Indeed, He would be stricken for the sins of humanity (Acts 8:32-33).

E. The Explanation Offered by Philip: vss. 34-35

The eunuch asked Philip, "Tell me, please, who is the prophet talking about, himself or someone else?" Then Philip began with that very passage of Scripture and told him the good news about Jesus.

The Ethiopian asked Philip whether Isaiah was talking about himself or someone else (Acts 8:34). What an opportunity this was to tell the good news about Christ! Philip explained how Jesus fulfilled the prophecy, namely, how He had been condemned and crucified as the Lamb of God (vs. 35).

First-century Jews did not speak much about a suffering Messiah. The Jewish people, facing the yoke of Roman rule, believed that the Messiah would come as the Lion of Judah, a delivering King, not a weak lamb. Many Jews have taught that the suffering one spoken of by Isaiah was the suffering nation of Israel.

We don't have the details of the conversation between Philip and the Ethiopian, but we may assume that Philip covered all the basics, including baptism. It was the Ethiopian, himself, not Philip, who noticed water along the way and proposed that he should be baptized (vs. 36). The official's question shows that he believed Jesus was indeed the fulfillment of Isaiah's prophecy.

Since the Ethiopian now believed in Jesus, he ordered his driver to stop his chariot. The vehicle referred to in verse 38 was probably an ox-drawn wagon. Most likely the Ethiopian was part of a caravan journeying in the same direction and moving slowly down the road.

Once the chariot had stopped, the official stepped into some nearby water and allowed Philip to baptize him. The baptism could have taken place at any number of locations. Tradition identifies the spot as near the town of Bethsura. The baptism, however, may have taken place nearer Gaza.

"When they came up out of the water, the Spirit of the Lord suddenly took Philip away" (vs. 39). Some see in this description a miracle in which Philip was transported from the site of the baptism to Azotus. Others, however, interpret this as merely Philip's abrupt departure under the compulsion of the Spirit. The biblical text leaves no doubt that Philip carried his preaching mission farther to the north (vs. 40).

The Ethiopian eunuch was not disturbed by Philip's sudden departure. He continued his journey, rejoicing in his new faith. Irenaeus, an early church leader who lived between A.D. 130–202, wrote that the official returned to Ethiopia and became a missionary to his own people.

The religious authorities had persecuted the church in order to halt the spread of the Gospel. Ironically, in causing Jesus' followers to scatter, the leaders in Jerusalem also caused the Gospel to spread far and wide. Now it had gone beyond the borders of Judea and Samaria.

Sometimes we have to become uncomfortable before we will move. We may not want to experience it, but discomfort may be the best thing for us because God may be working through our hurts. In the midst of painful circumstances, we may want to stop and ask whether God might be preparing us for a special task.

"Persecution"

Persecution is an opportunity for service, and Philip is given here as an example of an evangelist (Eph. 4:11). Called to be a deacon like Stephen before him, Philip discovered added spiritual gifts and became a mighty evangelist. He took the Gospel to Samaria, just as Christ had done in John 4; and thus for the first time in Acts we see the ministry of the Word moved from Jewish territory. Persecution only opened the door for soul-winning; what began as "great persecution" (vs.1) became "great joy" (vs. 8).

Discussion Questions

1. What anxieties and fears might Philip have had in preaching to the Samaritans?
2. What was the purpose of the miracles, signs, and wonders in promoting the Gospel?
3. Why was Philip a good choice to be the one to share the Gospel with the Ethiopian eunuch?
4. How do you think the conversion of the Ethiopian helped the spread of the Gospel?
5. What social barriers can hinder us from becoming more effective witnesses for Christ? How can we overcome them?
6. What opportunities to witness for Christ do you see in your community?

Now Ask Yourself . . .

Is my behavior and actions a witness to Christ in my life?

How can I improve my relationships with others who may have different beliefs than mine?

Illustrations

Philip was a groundbreaker. In Samaria he had to overcome whatever religious disagreements and racial prejudice he might have had regarding the Samaritans in order to proclaim the Gospel to them. Later he had to go beyond barriers of race and social class to tell the good news of Jesus to an Ethiopian official. Philip was obedient to God and overcame social barriers in the process.

Often Christians allow social differences to hinder their relationships with others. However, the command to spread the Gospel demands that we see all people as individuals of sacred worth and value, created in the image of God.

Venturing into new and unfamiliar social situations can be scary. The fear of being inadequate or rejected can make us feel powerless in sharing our faith in Christ. Nevertheless, we must never lose sight of the truth that God will be with us when we encounter social barriers and enable us to share the good news of Jesus with those who are different from us.

Our mission field may begin with our families, then extend into our neighborhood, and finally into the larger society. Whether we are chatting with our nonbelieving grandson, our Buddhist next-door neighbor, or the woman of another ethnic group sitting next to us at a ball game, we are to be alert to the opportunities to tell people how much Christ means to us.

Gentiles Receive the Spirit

Scripture

Background Scripture: *Acts 10:1—11:18*

Scripture Lesson: *Acts 10:30-39, 44-48*

Key Verse: *Then Peter began to speak: "I now realize how true it is that God does not show favoritism but accepts men from every nation who fear him and do what is right." Acts 10:34-35.*

Lesson Aim

To seek God's help in overcoming any personal prejudices that may be limiting our Christian witness.

Lesson Setting

Time: About A.D. 40

Place: Caesarea

Lesson Outline

Gentiles Receive the Spirit

   I. The Explanation of Cornelius: Acts 10:30-33

      A. *The Vision of the Angel: vss. 30-32*

      B. *The Openness of Cornelius: vs. 33*

  II. The Proclamation of the Word: Acts 10:34-39a

      A. *God's Acceptance of All Believers: vss. 34-35*

      B. *God's Message of Peace: vs. 36*

      C. *God's Anointing of Jesus: vss. 37-39a*

 III. The Bestowal of the Spirit: Acts 10:44-48

      A. *The Reception of the Spirit: vss. 44-46*

      B. *The Baptizing of the Gentile Converts:
         vss. 47-48*

Introduction

Called to Be Inclusive

Many of the personal prejudices of adults have been ingrained in them since childhood. On their own they don't have the determination and strength to overcome their deep-seated intolerances. Only God can remove those biases.

If there is any doubt about prejudice in the church, ask yourself why the statement "Sunday morning remains the most segregated time of the week" still rings true. Possibly members of your class are extremely alike. Can it be that personal prejudices have made it uncomfortable for other kinds of people to feel welcome?

This week's lesson encourages your students to seek God's help in overcoming whatever prejudices they have. This in turn will enable them to present a truly Christian witness to others.

Lesson Commentary

I. The Explanation of Cornelius: Acts 10:30-33

A. The Vision of the Angel: vss. 30-32

Cornelius answered: "Four days ago I was in my house praying at this hour, at three in the afternoon. Suddenly a man in shining clothes stood before me and said, ' Cornelius, God has heard your prayer and remembered your gifts to the poor. Send to Joppa for Simon who is called Peter. He is a guest in the home of Simon the tanner, who lives by the sea.' "

With the departure of Saul (Paul) to Tarsus, the narrative shifts once again to Peter. The apostle traveled to Lydda, healed a paralyzed man named Aeneas, and led many people to the Lord. Peter then traveled to Joppa and restored to life a woman name Dorcas. As a result, many trusted in Christ. Peter then remained in Joppa for some time with a man named Simon, who treated and tanned animal hides (Acts 9:32-43). Joppa was an ancient seaport on the Mediterranean Sea about 35 miles northwest of Jerusalem.

Meanwhile an angel appeared in a vision to a Roman centurion name Cornelius (10:1). He was a noncommissioned military officer in charge of about 100 men. Cornelius not only drilled his soldiers and inspected their weapons but also ensured they had adequate food and clothing.

Cornelius was stationed in Caesarea [SESS-uh-ree-uh]. This seaport on the Mediterranean coast was about 65 miles northwest of Jerusalem, and Tacitus called it the capital for the province of Judea. During his rule, Herod the Great refurbished the harbor at great expense. Caesarea contained the residences for the Roman governor of Judea as well as a regular Roman garrison.

In describing Cornelius as "God-fearing" (vs. 2), Luke used a common New Testament designation for a Gentile who believed in one God and in the ethics of Judaism, but who had not converted to Judaism. The piety of Cornelius is evident in his seeking the Lord through prayer, fasting, and good works. But these noble activities could not save him from sin.

Cornelius lacked one essential thing—a knowledge of Jesus as the Messiah. God honored the prayers of the centurion by dispatching an angel, who told him to send for Peter (vs. 5). Cornelius obeyed the angel's instructions by sending three men to escort the apostle to Caesarea (vss. 7-8).

God had spoken to Peter in a vision. While the apostle was praying on the roof of his guest's house, he fell into a trance and was commanded by God to eat certain ceremonially unclean animals. When Peter objected, the Lord declared that what He had made clean was no longer to be regarded as impure (vss. 9-15).

After the vision had ended and while Peter was reflecting on its significance, Cornelius' men arrived and asked for the apostle. Meanwhile the Spirit directed Peter to accompany them. The following day these men escorted Peter and some fellow Jews from Joppa to Caesarea (vss. 16-23).

When the group arrived, they found that Cornelius, his relatives, and his close friends had been waiting for them (vs. 24). The centurion told Peter that four days earlier he had been fasting and praying when he saw a vision of a man wearing "shining clothes" (vs. 30). This description indicates an angel.

The angel told Cornelius that God had listened to his prayers and seen how he helped others by giving "gifts to the poor" (vs. 31). The angel had instructed the centurion to invite Peter (whose primary name was Simon) to come to his home. The angel

"Cornelius"

Cornelius was a God-fearing Gentile who did not know the truth of the Gospel. He was devout, honest, generous, and sincere; but he was not a saved man. It is possible to be very religious but still be lost! Were it not for the fact that God in His grace spoke to Cornelius, he would never have become a believer. We see here a fulfillment of Christ's promise in John 7:17, "If any man is willing to do HIs will, he shall know the truth." An angel spoke to him and told him to send for Peter. Why did not the angel give Cornelius the message himself? Because God has not given to angels the ministry of sharing the Gospel to lost souls, a privilege angles cannot have!

87

promised Cornelius that Peter would come to Caesarea and speak to him about the Lord (vs. 32).

B. The Openness of Cornelius: vs. 33

"So I sent for you immediately, and it was good of you to come. Now we are all here in the presence of God to listen to everything the Lord has commanded you to tell us."

Cornelius thanked Peter and his companions for accepting his invitation. The centurion then indicated that he and his household were quite eager to listen to all that God wanted the apostle to say to them (Acts 10:33). This was an ideal opportunity for Peter to tell the Gospel to an eager and open Gentile audience.

II. The Proclamation of the Word: Acts 10:34-39

A. God's Acceptance of All Believers: vss. 34-35

Then Peter began to speak: "I now realize how true it is that God does not show favoritism but accepts men from every nation who fear him and do what is right."

The vision Peter had earlier experienced radically changed his perspective. As the apostle related in Acts 11:4, he saw something like a large sheet being let down by its four corners from the sky. When the apostle looked inside the sheet, he saw all sorts of creatures, which the Jews considered unlawful to eat. He also heard a voice command him to kill and eat these animals (vss. 5-7).

At first Peter protested, declaring that he had never eaten anything forbidden by Jewish law. But the voice from heaven declared that what God had identified as acceptable must not be regarded otherwise (vss. 8-9). The vision the apostle had experienced was intended by God to free him from his racial bigotry and personal prejudice against Gentiles.

In declaring in 10:34 that God "does not show favoritism," Peter meant that the Lord does not favor people because of their language, culture, economic level, educational attainments, gender, or nationality. Rather, in every nation God freely and unconditionally accepts those "who fear him and do what is right" (vs. 35).

It's clear that Cornelius fit this description. However, he had never heard the good news about Jesus, and that's why God sent Peter to proclaim the Gospel to him and his household.

B. God's Message of Peace: vs. 36

"You know the message God sent to the people of Israel, telling the good news of peace through Jesus Christ, who is Lord of all."

In the goodness and wisdom of God, He sent His Son, Jesus Christ, to the world as a Jew to minister among the Jewish people. Thus, the message of salvation first came to Israel (Rom. 1:16). When many rejected the good news, the truth was proclaimed to Gentiles as well as Jews so that all who trusted in Christ would be saved (John 1:12).

Peter declared that the Gospel was a message of peace through Christ (Acts 10:36). Jesus made peace possible between people and God (Rom. 5:1). Jesus also made peace possible between Jews and Gentiles (Eph. 2:14-18). This was a remarkable disclosure, something entirely unheard of before.

Peter then declared that Jesus "is Lord of all" (Acts 10:36). This truth has become a central tenet of the Christian faith. Since Jesus is Lord, all others must bow in homage to Him (Phil. 2:9-11). And because Jesus is Lord, all religious traditions and customs must be made subservient to His will.

C. God's Anointing of Jesus: vss. 37-39a

"You know what has happened throughout Judea, beginning in Galilee after the baptism that John preached—how God anointed Jesus of Nazareth with the Holy Spirit and power, and how he went around doing good and healing all who were under the power of the devil, because God was with him. We are witnesses of everything he did in the country of the Jews and in Jerusalem."

Peter proclaimed the message of the Gospel in a simple and direct manner. The apostle noted that after John the Baptist began preaching, Jesus ministered throughout Galilee and Judea (Acts 10:37). Christ did not do good works in His own power; rather, God anointed Him with "the Holy Spirit and power" (vs. 38). As God's Savior, Jesus performed works of healing and was victorious over Satan.

Peter declared that he and the other apostles were eyewitnesses of all Jesus did throughout Israel and in Jerusalem (vs. 39). For instance, Peter testified that religious authorities crucified the Messiah. Though Jesus died, God raised Him to life and allowed Him to appear, not to the general public, but to those whom the Lord had chosen beforehand to be His witnesses. They were the ones who ate and drank with the Savior after He rose from the dead (vss. 40-41).

Peter related that God had commissioned the apostles to proclaim Jesus as the Judge of all humankind, both "the living and the dead" (vs. 42). Jesus is the person whom all the Old Testament prophets testified about. Their central message was that by believing in Christ, people could have their sins forgiven (vs. 43). This truth applied to those listening to Peter. God wanted them to hear the good news and receive Christ by faith.

III. The Bestowal of the Spirit: Acts 10:44-48

A. The Reception of the Spirit: vss. 44-46

While Peter was still speaking these words, the Holy Spirit came on all who heard the message. The circumcised believers who had come with Peter were astonished that the gift of the Holy Spirit had been poured out even on the Gentiles. For they heard them speaking in tongues and praising God.

It's unclear exactly who was part of the household of Cornelius. In all probability, his household consisted of relatives and servants (see Acts 10:24; 16:33).

Peter's visit to Cornelius, the outpouring of the Spirit on the centurion and the rest of the Gentiles who heard Peter speak, and their tongues-speaking underscored that God wanted believers to proclaim the Gospel to all people, regardless of their station in life, their nationality, or their material possessions (10:44). The tongues-speaking that occurred at Caesarea was a sign to the believing Jews that the gift of the Spirit poured out on the saved Gentiles was in every respect equivalent to the gift poured out on them at Pentecost (vs. 46).

Acts 10:45 makes reference to the "circumcised believers." These were Jewish Christians from Joppa who had accompanied Peter to Caesarea (vs. 23). The apostle had exercised great forethought in bringing them along, for they would serve as confirming witnesses that "the gift of the Holy Spirit had been poured out even on the Gentiles" (vs. 45). In other words, God allowed these Gentiles to share alike with their fellow believing Jews in the benefits of redemption (11:17).

Even on the "Gentiles"

At this point the Spirit interrupted Peter and wrought a miracle in the hearts of these Gentiles. They believed the Word! And when they believed, the Spirit was poured out upon them, the evidence being that they spoke with tongues. The Jews with Peter were astonished that God would save the Gentiles without first making them Jewish proselytes. Let by the Spirit, Peter commanded that they be baptized; and Peter and his friends stayed and ate with these new believers.

Sadly, the early Jewish Christians initially did not realize that God had meant the Gospel for Gentiles as well as Jews. It's no wonder that Peter's Jewish companions were astonished at the outpouring of the Spirit on Cornelius and his household (10:45). It was one thing for God to seek Gentiles. But it was something else for Him not to require them to become ceremonially clean as full converts before He baptized them with the Spirit.

B. The Baptizing of the Gentile Converts: vss. 47-48

Then Peter said, "Can anyone keep these people from being baptized with water? They have received the Holy Spirit just as we have." So he ordered that they be baptized in the name of Jesus Christ. Then they asked Peter to stay with them for a few days.

In light of what God had done, how could Peter oppose the divine will (Acts 11:17)? That's why the apostle permitted Cornelius and his household to be "baptized with water" (10:47). After all, the believing Gentiles had received the Spirit in the same way as the believing Jews on the day of Pentecost (2:1-4).

The phrase "just as we have" (10:47) is worth further comment. God did not require any laying on of hands before He poured out the Spirit on the Gentiles. In this way, He put to rest the flawed notion that saved Gentiles had to convert to Judaism before they could belong to the church as the spiritual equals of saved Jews.

Peter accepted the request of the Gentile converts to stay with them a few more days, no doubt to teach them further about their faith in Christ (vs. 48). The apostle undoubtedly rejoiced in what God had done in bringing Gentiles to salvation.

Discussion Questions

1. How do the words of Cornelius to Peter show that the centurion had a heart that was open to God?
2. In what ways did both Cornelius and Peter obey God?
3. Why did Peter's personal testimony make his message more powerful?
4. What great change in God's dealings with humanity does this week's Scripture text show?
5. What things should you look for in other people when you are trying to overcome prejudice you might have toward them?
6. How can you help others in your church who have problems with prejudice toward some of those who need Christ?

Now Ask Yourself . . .

Do I look at others with my eyes or through the eyes of Jesus?

How can seeing people as Jesus sees them affect how I treat them?

Illustrations

Prejudice is a generalized fear of what we do not understand, and it causes us to avoid certain people who make us feel uncomfortable. Many of these "other" people we avoid are not Christians, and it is we who can tell them about the Lord. Because we refuse to associate with them, they become victims of our bias.

To become effective witnesses, we must deal honestly with ourselves. God's Spirit comes with light to expose our attitudes. His prodding, however, can be painful, as we may see things about ourselves that we don't like.

In diagnosing the problem of prejudice in our lives, we should ask ourselves some candid questions. Do we insist on worshiping only with people who are similar to us? Do we have hostile opinions of others just because they are radically different, economically deprived, or physically handicapped? Are the views we have about others based on truth, or exaggerations and mis-statements?

During Jesus' time on earth, He reached out to all sorts of people with the message of truth. Despite the disapproval of His peers, Jesus willingly ministered to Samaritans and Romans, to the poor and the infirm. As His followers, we too should display the love and kindness of God to whomever we encounter. With the Spirit's help, we can succeed in doing so!

The Church in Antioch

Scripture

Background Scripture: *Acts 11:19-30; 13:1-3*

Scripture Lesson: *Acts 11:19-30; 13:1-3*

Key Verse: *While they were worshiping the Lord and fasting, the Holy Spirit said, "Set apart for me Barnabas and Saul for the work to which I have called them."* *Acts 13:2.*

Lesson Aim

To promote a unity within the church body that transcends racial, ethnic, and cultural differences.

Lesson Setting

Time: About A.D. 44–46

Place: Syrian Antioch

Lesson Outline

The Church in Antioch

  I.   The Syrian Antioch Congregation: *Acts 11:19-30*
       A. *The Cosmopolitan Nature of the Church:*
       vss. 19-21
       B. *The Confirmation of the Church: vss. 22-26*
       C. *The Charity of the Church: vss. 27-30*
  II. The Selection of Barnabas and Saul: *Acts 13:1-3*
       A. *The Prophets and Teachers in the Church: vs. 1*
       B. *The Spirit's Directive: vs. 2*
       C. *The Disciples' Obedience: vs. 3*

Introduction

Reaching Out to Others

John would never be a stellar seminary professor, for he was not a skilled teacher. But he was amazingly effective in evangelism, and he even led his church's witness in the community.

John combined warmth and boldness in his outreach. He wasn't afraid to call on visitors or to go door-to-door to tell people about Jesus. John loved the Savior and the Gospel. It's no wonder that God used John to bring many unsaved people to faith in Christ. John would have felt right at home in the evangelistically-minded church at Syrian Antioch.

Not every believer can do what John did. But we can ask God to help us reach out to the unsaved with the love of Christ. God is not limited to one method of evangelism. Of foremost priority is our willingness to cross racial, ethnic, and cultural barriers with the Gospel. When we are open to the leading of the Spirit, He will bring across our path people who are hungry to know Him.

Lesson Commentary

I. The Syrian Antioch Congregation: Acts 11:19-30

A. The Cosmopolitan Nature of the Church: vss. 19-21

Now those who had been scattered by the persecution in connection with Stephen traveled as far as Phoenicia, Cyprus and Antioch, telling the message only to Jews. Some of them, however, men from Cyprus and Cyrene, went to Antioch and began to speak to Greeks also, telling them the good news about the Lord Jesus. The Lord's hand was with them, and a great number of people believed and turned to the Lord.

After the conversion of the Roman centurion and his Gentile friends, Peter was criticized by his fellow believers in Judea (Acts 11:1-3). But the apostle's explanation of what had happened prompted them to praise God for bringing salvation to the Gentiles (11:18). The seeds of a missionary outreach to the Gentiles was sown after Stephen's death. It's true that Philip had proclaimed the Gospel in Samaria, but Samaritans were part Jewish (8:4-8). And though Peter had shared the good news with Cornelius, he already worshiped the true God (10:2). For the first time, Syrian Antioch believers began to actively share the Gospel with pagan Gentiles (11:19-20).

When Stephen was martyred for his faith (7:59-60), many

Christians were forced to leave Jerusalem and go throughout the regions of Judea and Samaria (8:1). They also went to Phoenicia, Cyprus, and Antioch (11:19).

Phoenicia [foh-NEE-shuh] was the land north of Palestine on the eastern shore of the Mediterranean Sea. Cyprus is a large island in the Mediterranean Sea. It's eclipsed in size only by Sicily and Sardinia. Antioch was the capital of the Roman province of Syria. The city was situated on the east bank of the Orontes River, about 17 miles from the Mediterranean Sea and 300 miles north of Jerusalem. Barnabas and the apostle Paul used Syrian Antioch as the base for their missionary journeys into Asia Minor.

At first, the early Christians shared the Gospel only with Jews, perhaps because the disciples observed the Jewish regulations that prohibited them from associating with Gentiles (11:19). But thankfully some believers from Cyprus and Cyrene began preaching to Gentiles about the Savior (vs. 20).

Cyrene [sigh-REEN] was a city located in northern Africa. In New Testament times it was the capital of the Roman district of Cyrenaica. Cyrene was quite cosmopolitan, and was especially noted for its large Jewish population.

Antioch was also a cosmopolitan center and a crossroads for travel and commerce. The believers from Cyprus and Cyrene told Greek residents of Syrian Antioch about Jesus. God was pleased with their decision and blessed their efforts by bringing them many converts (vs. 21). Here we see the Lord working through the followers of Christ to bring the lost to faith.

B. The Confirmation of the Church: vss. 22-26

News of this reached the ears of the church at Jerusalem, and they sent Barnabas to Antioch. When he arrived and saw the evidence of the grace of God, he was glad and encouraged them all to remain true to the Lord with all their hearts. He was a good man, full of the Holy Spirit and faith, and a great number of people were brought to the Lord. Then Barnabas went to Tarsus to look for Saul, and when he found him, he brought him to Antioch. So for a whole year Barnabas and Saul met with the church and taught great numbers of people. The disciples were called Christians first at Antioch.

The ability of the Gospel to make deep inroads in Syrian Antioch was nothing short of a miracle. The city was the center of worship

---

"Grace"

In verse 23 we see for the first time the word "grace" is used in Acts with reference to salvation. Grace was to become Paul's great message in years to come. Note that these Gentiles were saved by grace (vs. 23) through faith (vs. 21). This is what Ephesians 2:8-9 teaches.

for several cults that promoted sexual immorality and other forms of evil common to pagan religions. It's no wonder that the interest of the believers in the Jerusalem congregation was aroused when they learned that many Gentiles were trusting in Christ for salvation (11:22).

The church leaders in Jerusalem did not send Peter and John, but rather chose Barnabas, the believer who had previously given so much to the congregation (4:37) and who had vouched for Saul (Paul) not long after his conversion (9:27). Barnabas had earned the respect and trust of the apostles, and that's why they dispatched him to Antioch to evaluate what was going on there.

Barnabas, "Son of Encouragement" (4:36), lived up to his name when he arrived in Antioch. What he saw bore the marks of genuine salvation among the Gentiles. He was convinced that God's grace was at work in a mighty way there (11:23).

Barnabas was filled with joy over the newfound faith of the Gentile converts and encouraged them to remain true to the Lord. Most likely Barnabas's teaching centered on God's forgiveness in Christ. Barnabas undoubtedly told the new believers what it means to follow God. And he assuredly underscored the importance of Jesus' life, death, and resurrection.

Barnabas soon realized that the needs of the new converts in Antioch exceeded his ability to shoulder alone. He thus traveled to Tarsus to find Saul. And after finding him, Barnabas brought him back to Antioch to help in the work of the ministry. They busied themselves in teaching large numbers of people about Jesus (vss. 25-26).

Luke noted that it was at Antioch that followers of Jesus were first called Christians. The disciples received this name because they worshiped and served Christ, the Messiah. Though enemies of the faith may have used the term to ridicule adherents of the Way, believers willingly adopted the label. King Herod Agrippa II knew about the term, for he used it when talking to the apostle Paul (26:28). The only other occurrence appears in 1 Peter 4:16.

At the Last Supper, Jesus prayed to the Father that His disciples would be one in faith and purpose (John 17:21, 23). This unity within the church body is evident in the way God's people in Antioch and Jerusalem ministered to each other. Their love and concern were not hindered by whether they were Jewish or Gentile, educated or uneducated, rich or poor.

Like the believers in Antioch and Jerusalem, Christians today can strive to promote unity among churches that are different racially, ethnically, and culturally. This kind of partnering, however, often requires some readjustment of attitudes.

Like Barnabas, we need to set aside stereotypes. He saw beyond Saul as a Pharisee to a person who could teach the Gentiles at Antioch. One way we can get rid of our preconceived ideas about others is by reflecting on what we all have in common in Christ. For instance, all believers are forgiven of sin, adopted into God's family, and made heirs of fabulous eternal riches. Because our oneness in Christ transcends race, ethnicity, and culture, so should our unity with the church body.

C.   The Charity of the Church: vss. 27-30

During this time some prophets came down from Jerusalem to Antioch. One of them, named Agabus, stood up and through the Spirit predicted that a severe famine would spread over the entire Roman world. (This happened during the reign of Claudius.) The disciples, each according to his ability, decided to provide help for the brothers living in Judea. This they did, sending their gift to the elders by Barnabas and Saul.

During this time, some prophets traveled from Jerusalem to Antioch (Acts 11:27). This is the first time in Acts that Luke mentioned believers with the gift of prophecy. This special ability involved both the prediction of future events and the proclamation of new special revelation.

One prophet in particular stood out. His name was Agabus. During one church meeting, he stood up and predicted by the Spirit that a severe famine would engulf the entire Roman world. Luke noted that this took place during the reign of the Roman emperor Claudius (A.D. 41–54; vs. 28). This serious food shortage occurred because of a drought that had extended across the Roman Empire for many years. Agabus also foretold that imprisonment and suffering awaited the apostle Paul in Jerusalem. Like the prophets of the Old Testament, Agabus used props (in this case Paul's belt) to illustrate his prediction (21:10-11).

By the fourth decade of the first century A.D., the members of the congregation in Antioch had become so well established that they decided to send relief money to the Christians in Judea. No one forced the believers in Antioch to be generous. Rather, they

---

"Famine"

This famine is important, for if we read Acts 2:44-45 and 4:31-35, we see that a vital change has taken place in the Jerusalem church. In Acts 2—7, the church at Jerusalem had no needs at all; in 11:27-30 we read that these same people were in need of outside help. What had happened? The "kingdom program" with its special blessings had passed on. As long as the kingdom was being offered to the Jews, the Spirit conferred special blessings on the believers, and there was not one that lacked among them. But when the kingdom was finally rejected with the stoning of Stephen, these unusual blessings were withdrawn, leaving the Jewish believers in need.

genuinely cared about the needs of their fellow believers in the Jerusalem church (vs. 29). This is the sort of cheerful giving that the Bible commends (2 Cor. 9:7).

The leaders in the Antioch congregation chose Barnabas and Saul to take their gifts to the elders of the church in Jerusalem (Acts 11:30). This is the first reference to elders in Acts. They were appointed to manage the affairs of the church and meet the spiritual needs of believers.

II. The Selection of Barnabas and Saul: Acts 13:1-3

A. The Prophets and Teachers in the Church: vs. 1

In the church at Antioch there were prophets and teachers: Barnabas, Simeon called Niger, Lucius of Cyrene, Manaen (who had been brought up with Herod the tetrarch) and Saul.

Luke noted that God had blessed the church at Antioch with prophets and teachers (13:1). While prophets mostly proclaimed divine revelation, teachers explained its meaning so that the disciples could understand and apply what they heard (Eph. 4:11).

Along with Barnabas and Saul, the Antioch church leadership team included three other members. We know nothing about these men beyond what we find in Acts 13:1. One of the men, Simeon, also bore the nickname "Niger" (meaning "black"), probably because of his skin color. Another, named Lucius [LOU-shuss], evidently had moved to Antioch from Cyrene. Two of the leaders were from Africa. About the third Antioch church leader, Manaen [MAN-ih-ehn], Luke noted that he "had been brought up with Herod the tetrarch." This has been variously interpreted to mean that he was a foster brother, childhood companion, or courtier of Herod Antipas.

B. The Spirit's Directive: vs. 2

While they were worshiping the Lord and fasting, the Holy Spirit said, "Set apart for me Barnabas and Saul for the work to which I have called them."

Under the leadership of the five believers, the Antioch Christians eagerly followed the Lord. For instance, they responded quickly when the Spirit revealed the church was to send out Barnabas and Saul as missionaries. This word from the Spirit, perhaps mediated through a local prophet, came while the congregation was engaged in worshiping and fasting (Acts 13:2).

This refreshing account has a dimension that can help us with our efforts in God's work. We should note that the Antioch believers did not hear God's message in a committee meeting or a strategy session. It was not because they set goals or established priorities that they sent out their first missionaries. Rather, they discerned God's will while they were worshiping and fasting.

There's nothing wrong with committees or goal setting. Indeed, we should use every possible means to accomplish God's purposes, including organization and administration. But the God-exalting worship dimension illustrated by the Antioch church must always be in the foreground.

As the Spirit instructed, the Antioch congregation set apart Barnabas and Saul for a special purpose. The concept of setting apart someone was familiar to the Jews. Rituals of the tabernacle and temple called for many articles to be sanctified and consecrated (Exod. 30:25-29). Such items were holy, reserved only for worship and never for common, everyday activities. Similarly, the two missionaries were to be set apart.

C. The Disciples' Obedience: vs. 3
So after they had fasted and prayed, they placed their hands on them and sent them off.

After further prayer and fasting, the church leaders obeyed the Holy Spirit and sent Barnabas and Saul on their way. The members of the congregation yielded their two veteran and beloved teachers to God's will. Implicit in the church's obedience was the knowledge that the Lord would use Barnabas and Saul to advance the Gospel to more cities beyond Antioch.

The Antioch church was the first to aggressively evangelize Gentiles. Clearly, this was a witnessing, worshiping, and giving assembly. Because the congregation included believers from different backgrounds, the church obediently heeded God's call to spread the Gospel beyond the confines of Jerusalem and Judea to the farthest reaches of the Roman world.

Discussion Questions

1. How did the persecution of the Christians in Jerusalem contribute to the spread of the Gospel?
2. In what ways do you think the character of Barnabas helped the Antioch church?
3. What attributes do you think Barnabas spotted in Saul that convinced him that Saul would be a good partner?
4. Do you think it is rare today for one church to give financial resources to another? If so, why?
5. What can churches do to build relationships with other congregations of other ethnic groups?
6. In what ways can people in your church support missionaries and evangelists?

Now Ask Yourself . . .

Have I examined my heart lately? If so, what condition is it in?

How can I show others in my church and community the love and compassion of Jesus?

Illustrations

It's tragic that churches fight and split over racial, ethnic, and cultural differences. Instead of taking the time to truly understand each other, Christians embrace stereotyped opinions and make exaggerated claims about believers who are different from them. The result is hurt feelings and hardened attitudes within the body of Christ.

Jesus challenges us to become people with tender hearts, unwilling to separate ourselves from believers who are racially, ethnically, or culturally different from us. We are to look at the hearts of others, soften our own hearts, and work for unity.

As we become increasingly tenderhearted, we will want to reach out to our fellow Christians in their times of need. The racial, ethnic, and cultural background of a brother or sister in the faith will not matter, especially as we seek to love and help them unconditionally. Our displays of compassion will be key factors in promoting unity within the church.

The Jerusalem Conference

Scripture
Background Scripture: *Acts 15:1-35*
Scripture Lesson: *Acts 15:1-2, 6-15, 19-20*
Key Verse: *"No! We believe it is through the grace of our Lord Jesus that we are saved, just as they are." Acts 15:11*

Lesson Aim
To be prepared to reply to current false teachings about salvation.

Lesson Setting
Time: A.D. 49 or 50
Place: Jerusalem

Lesson Outline
The Jerusalem Conference
  I. The Argument for Works: Acts 15:1-2
      A. *Gentile Circumcision Demanded: vs. 1*
      B. *A Delegation Sent to Jerusalem: vs. 2*
  II. The Argument for Grace: Acts 15:6-12
      A. *Peter's Work among the Gentiles: vss. 6-7*
      B. *God's Acceptance of the Gentiles: vss. 8-9*
      C. *Salvation by Grace Alone: vss. 10-11*
      D. *Barnabas and Paul's Testimony: vs. 12*
  III. The Decision for Grace: Acts 15:13-15, 19-20
      A. *Affirming Peter's Remarks: vss. 13-14*
      B. *Acknowledging the Teaching of Scripture: vs. 15*
      C. *Welcoming Believing Gentiles: vss. 19-20*

Introduction

Defending the Truth

Jesus offers salvation with no strings attached. But because it seems too simplistic or too available to everyone, some people have attempted to place other conditions on becoming a part of God's family. Attending church regularly, being more good than bad, and having good parents have been cited as a means of earning our way into heaven. Such heresy can quickly move into the church.

Most of your students probably have encountered people who have asserted such false teachings about salvation. Whether students have heard it from a member of a cult or discussed it with a neighbor or co-worker, they probably all wished that they had been better prepared to reply to the other person's comments about salvation. This week's lesson will help them be better prepared the next time.

Lesson Commentary

I. The Argument for Works: Acts 15:1-2

A. Gentile Circumcision Demanded: vs. 1

Some men came down from Judea to Antioch and were teaching the brothers: "Unless you are circumcised, according to the custom taught by Moses, you cannot be saved."

After returning from their missionary journey, Paul and Barnabas spent time with the church in Syrian Antioch reporting all that God had done through them. The success of their mission no doubt brought joy to the believers who had sent them.

The entrance of so many Gentiles into the church, however, caused problems for a number of Jewish believers in Judea. Thus some from within the group of Jewish Christians came to Antioch and began arguing that circumcision was necessary in order to be saved (Acts 15:1).

God instituted circumcision as a sign of the covenant between Himself and Abraham's descendants (Gen. 17:9-14). This covenant sign was intended to mark their entry into the community of faith in Yahweh (the Hebrew word for "Lord"). In New Testament times, circumcision and uncircumcision were used as metaphors for the spiritual condition of the heart. A heart that was desensitized to the things of God was called uncircumcised, whereas a heart that was fully devoted to the Lord was called circumcised.

B. A Delegation Sent to Jerusalem: vs. 2

This brought Paul and Barnabas into sharp dispute and debate with them. So Paul and Barnabas were appointed, along with some other believers, to go up to Jerusalem to see the apostles and elders about this question.

The message that faith is not enough for receiving salvation set off a heated discussion (Acts 15:2). We can be sure that the arguments of Paul and Barnabas were packed with intensity and emotion as they defended the doctrine of grace. In other words, God did the entire work of salvation and believers can do nothing to merit God's favor (Eph. 2:8-9).

Because the Christians at Syrian Antioch were not able to resolve the issue on their own, they decided to send a delegation—which included Paul and Barnabas—to Jerusalem. The presence of the apostles and other prominent Christian leaders in Jerusalem provided the opportunity for the issue to be discussed and decided at the highest level. Undoubtedly, the way they resolved the matter would be regarded as official by the majority of Jesus' followers.

As the delegation from the Antioch church traveled through Phoenicia and Samaria, believers in these regions rejoiced at the news that Gentiles had trusted in Christ (vs. 3). This good will also may have helped build a broader base of support for the side favoring salvation by grace alone.

After arriving in Jerusalem, the delegation was welcomed by the apostles, elders, and other members in the church. When Paul, Barnabas, and their colleagues reviewed what God had done through them, some of the believing Pharisees argued that Gentiles had to be circumcised and observe the laws of Moses (vss. 4-5). This was a serious matter that threatened to divide the unity of believing Jews and Gentiles.

From these verses we see that Paul wasn't the only Pharisee to convert to the Christian faith. But unlike Paul, the Pharisees at the council had not made a clean break with their past. They had been taught that righteousness comes through obedience to the law, and they still believed it. They continued to look down on people who didn't observe the customs and rites of their religious tradition.

"Dispute"

Whenever God's work is progressing, Satan begins to oppose it, and he usually works through lies. The reason many churches are ineffective today is because they believe "religious lies" instead of God's Word. Certain Pharisees from the Jerusalem church had gone to Antioch and told the Gentile Christians that their salvation was not valid unless they were circumcised and obeyed the law of Moses. Paul and Barnabas disputed with them, and it was decided to take the issue to the apostles and elders in Jerusalem.

II. The Argument for Grace: Acts 15:6-12

A. Peter's Work among the Gentiles: vss. 6-7

The apostles and elders met to consider this question. After much discussion, Peter got up and addressed them: "Brothers, you know that some time ago God made a choice among you that the Gentiles might hear from my lips the message of the gospel and believe."

Since the apostles and elders had no written New Testament to turn to, they hammered out doctrine on the anvil of practical experience, guided by the Old Testament, the teachings of Jesus, and the illuminating ministry of the Spirit. The participants discussed the issue openly and at length, as all churches should do when debating a controversial matter (Acts 15:6).

Peter, it seems, delivered the decisive speech. He began by reminding those present of how God had used him to bring about the conversion of Cornelius and his household (vs. 7). Though most of the leaders knew the details of what had happened, Peter's retelling of the event demonstrated that God had settled the controversy about the inclusion of Gentiles years earlier.

B. God's Acceptance of the Gentiles: vss. 8-9

God, who knows the heart, showed that he accepted them by giving the Holy Spirit to them, just as he did to us. He made no distinction between us and them, for he purified their hearts by faith.

Peter noted that he had been the first to bear witness to God's work among the Gentiles. In response to the Lord's command to go to the house of Cornelius, Peter proclaimed the Gospel to the people gathered in the centurion's home and they believed the message. God responded by pouring out His Spirit on them before the apostle had even finished speaking (Acts 15:8).

Drawing conclusions from what God had done in the household of Cornelius, Peter made four observations. First, the real test of salvation should be the condition of a person's heart, which God alone knows. Second, God proved that He accepted believing Gentiles by giving them the Holy Spirit. Third, God did not distinguish between those who were circumcised and those who were uncircumcised. Last, God did not lower His standards. He gave His Spirit to all those He had made pure through faith in Christ (vs. 9).

Peter had a reputation for observing the laws of Moses and for being a personal disciple of the risen Lord. The apostle thus was a credible and convincing witness to his peers. If Peter claimed that Jews and Gentiles were saved by God's grace, the Christian leaders could accept what he said as true.

C. Salvation by Grace Alone: vss. 10-11
"Now then, why do you try to test God by putting on the necks of the disciples a yoke that neither we nor our fathers have been able to bear? No! We believe it is through the grace of our Lord Jesus that we are saved, just as they are."

Peter knew that he was not saved because of anything he had done. In fact, he argued that the law's demands were a burden too heavy for anyone to bear (Acts 15:10). The apostle asked how his peers could impose that burden on Gentile believers when they couldn't carry it themselves. Peter concluded by stating that both Jews and Gentiles were saved by God's grace. There was no difference (vs. 11).

Paul similarly noted that God has a way of providing righteousness, and it is apart from the law. Of course, the entire Old Testament bears witness to the fact that being justified in God's eyes cannot occur from keeping the law. God treats everyone alike. He views people as being acceptable in His sight only when they trust in Christ for salvation. All must come to God through Christ, for all have sinned and fallen short of God's glory (Rom. 3:21-23).

God freely justifies people by His grace, and His justification is made available through the redemption from sin that Christ purchased at Calvary. The Lord offered His Son on the cross as an atoning sacrifice for sins. Christ shed His blood so that by faith in Him we could come to God. The Lord did this to show that in the past He was right and fair to be patient and not punish people for their sins. Similarly, we see that God is justified when He declares people to be upright on the basis of their faith in Christ (vss. 24-26).

D. Barnabas and Paul's Testimony: vs. 12
The whole assembly became silent as they listened to Barnabas and Paul telling about the miraculous signs and wonders God had done among the Gentiles through them.

Barnabas and Paul picked up the thread of Peter's arguments, and the entire assembly listened in silence as the two spoke. They declared that God had given them the ability to perform miracles and signs among the Gentiles and to lead many to faith in Christ (Acts 15:12). This fact proved that what had happened with Cornelius was not a fluke. God was still making it clear that He was giving grace to Gentiles without requiring them to obey the laws of Moses.

III. The Decision for Grace: Acts 15:13-15, 19-20

"James Spoke"

Paul and his party were the next witnesses, and their reports of God's work among the Gentiles completely silenced the opposition. Then James took the floor and gave the final decision. This James is the Lord's brother who had become the leader of the Jerusalem church in Peter's place. His words in vss. 14-21 must be understood if the church is to carry on God's program in this age.

A. Affirming Peter's Remarks: vss. 13-14
When they finished, James spoke up: "Brothers, listen to me. Simon has described to us how God at first showed his concern by taking from the Gentiles a people for himself."

After another period of discussion among those present at the Jerusalem council, everyone stopped talking. James, the half brother of the Lord and the one presiding over the meeting, made a statement to his colleagues (Acts 15:13).

James had become virtually a moderator of the church in Jerusalem because of his outstanding character and piety. Tradition says that his knees were like those of camels because he had spent so much time kneeling in prayer. He also had a reputation as a rigorous keeper of the law, which probably made the legalists confident that he would decide in their favor.

James began by referring to Peter's description of how God had taken the initiative in bringing Gentiles into the church. James must have stunned the legalists when he said that God had "taken from the Gentiles a people for himself" (vs. 14). In times past the latter part of the phrase had been reserved for Israel. But James was declaring that God had spiritually united saved Jews and Gentiles under the lordship of Christ.

B. Acknowledging the Teaching of Scripture: vs. 15
"The words of the prophets are in agreement with this."

James cited Amos 9:11-12 to drive home his point (Acts 15:16-18). Amos had foretold that God would one day rebuild and set up the ruined temple. This implied that the Israelites would be restored to a place of prominence. Amos also predicted that one day the rest of humanity would seek the Lord and that Gentiles as well as Jews would be among the redeemed (vss. 16-17).

The point being made by James was clear to his audience. The prophets had foreseen a day when both Jews and Gentiles would be included in the believing community and share in the messianic blessing. From eternity past God had decided to bring about this tremendous work of grace (vs. 18).

C. Welcoming Believing Gentiles: vss. 19-20

"It is my judgment, therefore, that we should not make it difficult for the Gentiles who are turning to God. Instead we should write to them, telling them to abstain from food polluted by idols, from sexual immorality, from the meat of strangled animals and from blood."

James concluded by stating that the council should not require Gentile converts to be circumcised to be saved (Acts 15:19). He also urged the council to ask Gentile believers to abstain from four behaviors that would be particularly offensive to Jews (vs. 20). James knew that if Gentile Christians showed a total disregard for the law in these areas, relations with their Jewish neighbors would become strained.

The determination of the council was summarized in a letter and delivered by the hands of Barnabas and Saul, along with Judas (surnamed Barsabbas) and Silas, to the Gentile believers (vss. 22-29). When the disciples in the congregation at Syrian Antioch learned what had been decided, they rejoiced. After Judas and Silas encouraged the disciples, Judas returned to Jerusalem. However, Silas remained behind to assist Paul and Barnabas in the work of the ministry (vss. 30-35).

Discussion Questions

1. Why were the religious legalists eager for the Gentile converts to observe the Mosaic laws?
2. Why did Paul and Barnabas react so strongly to the teaching of the legalists?
3. What do you think was Peter's strongest argument against imposing circumcision on Gentile converts? Why?
4. Why did James provide a confirmation from Scripture of his decision?
5. What are some of the false teachings about salvation that you have heard?
6. Why is Scripture a better test of truth than experience?

Now Ask Yourself . . .

Do I test what I hear from preachers and teachers with the Word of God?

Am I able to discern falsehoods when I hear them?

How can I keep informed so that I am not easily persuaded or deceived by false prophets or by modern-day religious cults?

Illustrations

How can Christians be prepared to reply to current false teachings about salvation? First, we should be immersed in what Scripture has to say about salvation. We should be able to turn to the key passages in the Bible that point to Christ as the only one who can save us or that teach that salvation is a gift of God (Acts 4:12; Eph. 2:8-9).

Second, we can study the writings of Christians who are experts on world religions, cults, and current religious movements. These Christians have spent years examining false doctrines about salvation and evangelizing people who are captives of these doctrines.

Third, we can go out of our way to talk with people who hold false teachings about salvation. At first we might want to bring a knowledgeable Christian friend along for encouragement and support. Eventually we will feel comfortable talking to unsaved people on our own. The more times we do it, the more ready we will be. And most importantly, perhaps some will come to accept Jesus as their Savior.

The Word at Work . . .

*W*hat would you do if you wanted to share God's love with children on the streets of your city? That's the dilemma David C. Cook faced in 1870s Chicago. His answer was to create literature that would capture children's hearts.

Out of those humble beginnings grew a worldwide ministry that has used literature to proclaim God's love and disciple generation after generation. Cook Communications Ministries is committed to personal discipleship—to helping people of all ages learn God's Word, embrace his salvation, walk in his ways, and minister in his name.

Opportunities—and Crisis

We live in a land of plenty—including plenty of Christian literature! But what about the rest of the world? Jesus commanded, "Go and make disciples of all nations" (Matt. 28:19) and we want to obey this commandment. But how does a publishing organization "go" into all the world?

There are five times as many Christians around the world as there are in North America. Christian workers in many of these countries have no more than a New Testament, or perhaps a single shared copy of the Bible, from which to learn and teach.

We are committed to sharing what God has given us with such Christians.

A vital part of Cook Communications Ministries is our international outreach, Cook Communications Ministries International (CCMI). Your purchase of this book, and of other books and Christian-growth products from Cook, enables CCMI to provide Bibles and Christian literature to people in more than 150 languages in 65 countries.

Cook Communications Ministries is a not-for-profit, self-supporting organization. Revenues from sales of our books, Bible curriculum, and other church and home products not only fund our U.S. ministry, but also fund our CCMI ministry around the world. One hundred percent of donations to CCMI go to our international literature programs.

. . . Around the World

CCMI reaches out internationally in three ways:

· Our premier International Christian Publishing Institute (ICPI) trains leaders from nationally led publishing houses around the world to develop evangelism and discipleship materials to transform lives in their countries.

· We provide literature for pastors, evangelists, and Christian workers in their national language. We provide study helps for pastors and lay leaders in many parts of the world, such as China, India, Cuba, Iran, and Vietnam.

· We reach people at risk—refugees, AIDS victims, street children, and famine victims—with God's Word. CCMI puts literature that shares the Good News into the hands of people at spiritual risk—people who might die before they hear the name of Jesus and are transformed by his love.

Word Power—God's Power

Faith Kidz, RiverOak, Honor, Life Journey, Victor, NexGen — every time you purchase a book produced by Cook Communications Ministries, you not only meet a vital personal need in your life or in the life of someone you love, but you're also a part of ministering to José in Colombia, Humberto in Chile, Gousa in India, or Lidiane in Brazil. You help make it possible for a pastor in China, a child in Peru, or a mother in West Africa to enjoy a life-changing book. And because you helped, children and adults around the world are learning God's Word and walking in his ways.

Thank you for your partnership in helping to disciple the world. May God bless you with the power of his Word in your life.

For more information about our international ministries, visit www.ccmi.org.